The
Orb
Project

The Orb Project

Míceál Ledwith, D.D., LL.D.
&
Klaus Heinemann, Ph.D.

Foreword by William A. Tiller, Ph.D.

ATRIA BOOKS
New York London Toronto Sydney

BEYOND WORDS
PUBLISHING

ATRIA BOOKS
A Division of Simon & Schuster, Inc.
1230 Avenue of the Americas
New York, NY 10020

BEYOND WORDS
PUBLISHING
20827 N.W. Cornell Road, Suite 500
Hillsboro, Oregon 97124-9808
503-531-8700 / 503-531-8773 fax
www.beyondword.com

Copyright © 2007 by Míceál Ledwith and Klaus Heinemann

Editor: Julie Steigerwaldt
Managing editor: Lindsay S. Brown
Copyeditor: Donna M. Rivera
Proofreader: Marvin Moore
Cover/interior design: Jerry Soga and Sara E. Blum
Composition: William H. Brunson Typography Services

First Atria Books/Beyond Words paperback edition November 2007

ATRIA BOOKS and colophon are trademarks of Simon & Schuster, Inc.
Beyond Words Publishing is a division of Simon & Schuster, Inc.

For more information about special discounts for bulk purchases,
please contact Simon & Schuster Special Sales at 1-800-456-6798 or
business@simonandschuster.com.

Manufactured in the United States of America

10 9 8 7 6 5 4 3

Library of Congress Cataloging-in-Publication Data

Ledwith, Míceál.
    The Orb Project / Míceál Ledwith & Klaus Heinemann ; foreword by William Tiller.
        p. cm.
    Includes bibliographical references.
    1. Spirit photography. I. Heinemann, Klaus. II. Title.

BF1381.L43   2007
133.9′2—dc22

2007010752

ISBN-13: 978-1-58270-182-0
ISBN-10:   1-58270-182-2

The corporate mission of Beyond Words Publishing, Inc.: *Inspire to Integrity*

Dedication

To those who search for an understanding of reality and our place in it.

Contents

Foreword by William A. Tiller   *ix*

Preface   *xxvii*

• • •

Part I: The Orb Phenomenon
    Míceál Ledwith, D.D., LL.D.   *1*

Foreword to Part I by JZ Knight   *3*

Introduction: "There Are More Things in Heaven
    and on Earth...."   *7*

1. *A Photographic Journey of Discovery*   *15*

2. *The Significance of Orb Coloring*   *27*

3. *Enormous Variety of Orb Manifestation*   *43*

4. *Vortices and Torsion Fields: Orbs That May Not*
    Be Electromagnetic   *53*

5. *Tips for Photographing Orbs*   *61*

6. *Distinguishing False Orb Pictures from Real*   *71*

7. *Orbs and Our Place in the Cosmos*   *77*

Part II: Orbs—Evidence of Divine Presence?

Klaus Heinemann, Ph.D.   *83*

Acknowledgments   *85*

Introduction: We Are Surrounded by a Cloud
  of Witnesses   *87*

 8. The Evidence   *95*

 9. Taking a Closer Look   *119*

10. Understanding the Findings   *141*

Afterword: Spirit Emanations and
  Spirit-directed Healing   *159*

Bibliography   *173*

• • •

Authors' Conclusion   *175*

Foreword

I have been asked to write this foreword by two gentlemen whom I highly respect, both as humans and for their many accomplishments in their respective professional fields. In this book, they meet and share their private, avocational, photographic studies on a very recent world phenomenon called "orbs." These orbs have been photographed at night with flash and in daylight with and without flash, mostly with digital cameras, by tens of thousands of people.

Many people think that orbs are physical entities, others think that they are spirit entities, and still others think that they are merely artifacts associated with light scattering from airborne particulates.

I have an extensive background in both traditional science and psychoenergetic science and had a decade-long "dance" in the 1970s with anomalous photographic phenomena (Kirlian photography and Stanislav O'Jack), so perhaps it is reasonable that I "throw my hat into the ring" on this one and add my perspective to the unfolding adventure.

After carefully reading the material provided by Míceál Ledwith, D.D., LL.D., and Klaus Heinemann, Ph.D., I am most impressed. After reflecting for some months on the data and my own psychoenergetic science modeling of nature, I have come to the conclusion that the appearance of "orbs" in and around the planet Earth at this time is not *accidental*. My intuitive view is that it is a part of a heightening of awareness brought about partially by the elevation in human thinking and partially by the increase in energies directed toward this planet by mostly benign life-forms existing in both traditional and untraditional (unseen) dimensions. My working hypothesis is that the orb phenomenon should be looked at as a positive experience for humanity, as just the first of a variety of communication manifestations to appear in the unfolding adventure of our future.

I think that it would benefit everyone to read this book. If the reader is willing to be tolerant with my technical perspective, I will tell you why.

The Tiller Perspective

First, we need to ask, "How does psychoenergetic science differ from traditional science?" For the past four hundred years, traditional science has not considered human consciousness as a significant thermodynamic variable in the study of natural phenomena. Rather, its investigations have orbited around the metaphorical reaction equation

$$MASS \leftrightarrow ENERGY \qquad (1)$$

with the major quantitative connection between these two being the Einstein Relationship, $E=MC^2$ (E=Energy, M=Mass, and C=velocity of electromagnetic light in physical vacuum). On the other hand, psychoenergetic science expands equation 1 to include human consciousness as a significant thermodynamic variable in the study of nature. However, our present difficulty is that there is no presently accepted definition of consciousness that is sufficiently quantitative to be broadly acceptable as the next term on the right of equation 1. Thus, let us not ask what consciousness *is* but instead ask what consciousness *does*. When we do this, we immediately see that consciousness manipulates *information*, whether via sums or products to get useful results; whether via random letters to make words; whether via mathematical symbols to make equations, or whether via the assembly of an array of puzzle pieces to make a beautiful picture. Further, for the past sixty to seventy years we have known that an increase in information content (in terms of bits) via a particular process in nature is quantitatively connected to a decrease in entropy (in terms of calories per degree centigrade) for the universe and, for the past one hundred and fifty years, we have known that the master potential function of thermodynamics, which drives all processes in nature, is the free energy per unit volume or per mole of chemical species and, in this function, entropy is on par with energy. Thus, the metaphorical reaction equation governing psychoenergetic science is

$$MASS \leftrightarrow ENERGY \leftrightarrow INFORMATION \leftrightarrow CONSCIOUSNESS \quad (2)$$

To make equation 2 a little more tangible, in traditional science of the past century we have built very large particle accelerators to collide streams of particles at high kinetic energy with each other in order to split some apart into smaller and more basic components so as to understand the subcomponents of all matter. In the now and in the future, we will use directed consciousness to manipulate information resident at different levels of reality in order to alter the properties of materials. This constitutes a shift in the thermodynamic free energy function of nature away from energy-induced changes to entropy-induced changes. In this, we will also see the importance of shifting from analogue information to digital information.

Next, I think it is important to say a little about human psychophysiology in order to see how malleable we are to our belief system and to both our unconscious and conscious intentions. Let us start with a bare statement of the "Psychophysiological Principle" and follow this with three biofeedback examples.

> *Every change in the human physiological state is accompanied by an*
> *appropriate change in the mental-emotional state, conscious or uncon-*
> *scious, and conversely every change in the human mental-emotional state,*
> *conscious or unconscious, is accompanied by an appropriate change in*
> *the physiological state.*

One of the most striking unconscious biofeedback experiments was carried out in the mid-1930s by Slater, involving the use of his "upside-down" glasses.[1] Subjects were asked to continually wear glasses that distorted perception so that the wearer saw everything in an upside-down configuration. It was very destabilizing for these subjects, but they did so. After two to three weeks (depending on the particular subject), there was a "flip": they suddenly saw everything "right side up" with the glasses on, and thereafter continued to do so. Then, when the subjects removed these glasses, the world suddenly appeared upside down again for another two to three weeks, depending on the individual, before normal vision was suddenly restored.

From the foregoing data, my working hypothesis is that the apparent disparity between the conventional worldview and the special glasses' inverted view somehow caused a force on the brain's dendrites to first construct some type of weakly hard-wired internal *inversion mirror* so that one's expectations were fulfilled and then later dissolve this brain structure element when it was no longer needed.

Stewart Wolf, M.D., did a double-blind study with a group of pregnant women suffering from nausea and vomiting.[2] He did it in two steps. First, he gave an antiemetic to one portion of the group and a placebo to the other. He was surprised to find how many of the women in the second group had a cessation of nausea and vomiting. In the second step, he took the placebo subgroup and gave them what he said was a very new and strong antiemetic. He observed that all of the women in this group overcame their nausea and vomiting. What he didn't tell them was that he actually gave them ipecac, a very strong emetic that is regularly used in hospital emergency rooms to induce vomiting. This is a truly remarkable psychophysiological result: the strength of the women's intention field created a thermodynamic force in their body that significantly exceeded the opposite sign force, the strong chemical force known to be present due to ipecac ingestion.

In the mid-1990s, I worked with colleagues at the Institute of Heart Math in California studying the effects of focusing intentional appreciation for someone or something (poem, painting, nature scene, and so on) through the heart on the electrophysiological state of humans.[3] The core biofeedback measurement instrument was the electrocardiogram (EKG) with subsidiary measurements of respiration (R), pulse transit time (PTT), and the electroencephalograph (EEG). The EKG data was automatically converted to heart rate variability (HRV) and displayed for the viewer in real time. Its power spectrum was also obtained. The time-trigger for invoking the onset of focused appreciation was labeled "Freezeframe." Figure 1 illustrates both the real-time changes in HRV plus the HRV power spectrum both before and after the freezeframe intention. Figure 2 provides power spectra

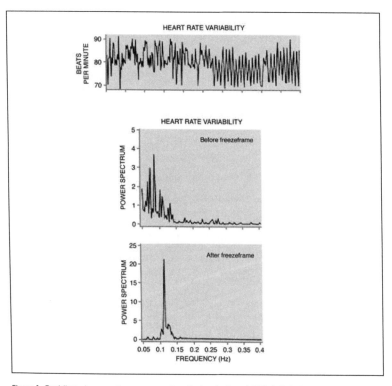

Figure 1. Real-time changes plus power spectrum for heart rate variability both before and after the freeze-frame intention.

data for all four simultaneous measurement systems before and after freezeframe onset. What we learn from this data is that the onset of a sincere appreciation focus through the heart brings (a) a state of internal coherence in the real-time HRV measurement; (b) a collapse of both the parasympathetic (high frequency) and sympathetic (low frequency) power spectrum HRV data to the baroreflex frequency

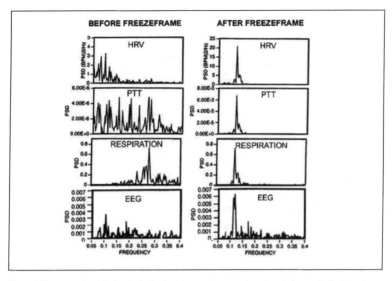

Figure 2. Power spectra data for all electrophysiology measurement systems before and after freezeframe onset (note the different vertical scales).

of 0.14 hertz, where the heart interacts strongly with the brain; and (c) strong entrainment of all four electrophysiological systems to this baroreflex frequency.

When one regularly practices this freezeframe/sincere appreciation technique, one also notes a significant change in the chemical factory output for the body—i.e., DHEA (the precursor to most body hormones) production increases while cortisol (the major stress chemical) production decreases. Thus, internal stress signatures are decreasing while beneficial hormones are increasing. All of the foregoing signifies an appreciably healthier human via this particular act of directed consciousness.

It is also interesting to note that, for individuals who are well-practiced in their ability to enter and sustain the entrainment mode or internal coherence mode of heart function while simultaneously intending to influence the molecular conformation of DNA molecules in a beaker of water located two to four feet *away* from their body, ultraviolet spectroscopy data shows that they can either unwind, or wind more tightly, the DNA strands at will.[3] If such a change can be made to occur to DNA located *outside* the body, imagine what could happen to DNA strands of the individual's cells located *inside* the body through their focused intentions.

Let me now provide an example of human biofield effects on the photographic process from a very internally well-developed human by the name of Stanislav O'Jack.

In the mid 1970s this very spiritually evolved gentleman came to see me at Stanford in order to learn what I thought about some photographs he had taken. Stan had grown up thinking that he was something of a "klutz" with cameras because when people would hand him their camera to take their picture, something a little strange would appear in the picture. Eventually, Stan observed a strong correlation between a feeling (sensation) in his seventh cervical plus fourth thoracic vertebrae and the appearance of strange phenomena appearing on the developed film. He showed me ten to twenty of his photographs to illustrate his point. He was using Kodak Kodacolor film, standard Kodak processing, and a simple Kodak camera with a plastic lens. His usual procedure was to place the camera stably on a tripod and trip it via a two-foot-long shutter-release mechanism.

Some of Stan's photos are shown in chapter 1 of Science and Human Transformation.[4] The photos showed the expected scene but with an overlay of (1) snake-like tubes of light, (2) contrails of light with a sea horse–like figure on the end, (3) floating open books, (4) floating bunches of banana-like structures, etc. Stan could obtain such photographs with other people's cameras but he needed to carry such a camera next to his body for several days to sensitize it to his biofield before he tried to take pictures. If he passed a sensitized camera to someone else, that person could take such pictures for the next one to ten hours. After that, no anomalous images would be present in the pictures. It seemed as if his biofield was necessary to keep the process "pumped up" so that such anomalous results became commonplace.

On learning all of this, I was very intrigued and designed a dual-camera experiment to do with Stan. A tripod platform was constructed to hold the two cameras at a twelve-inch separation and a special shutter-release mechanism created to open the two shutters simultaneously. Because we could no longer purchase a duplicate of Stan's favorite Kodak camera, we used a Minolta as the unsensitized camera on the tripod. The film in both cameras was standard Kodacolor, the processing was standard Kodak, and Stan was never allowed to touch the film roll. Someone else always loaded and unloaded the camera and sent the film away for processing.

Figures 3 and 4 show two of the astonishing dual-camera photos, with the Minolta on the left. In figure 3, the Minolta records the presence of one man and two ladies standing on stage in front of a blackboard; the Kodak shows us a semitransparent man through which we can see the blackboard. In addition, some kind of "stuff"

Figure 3. Example from the dual camera study: unsensitized camera result (left) and sensitized camera result (right). Note the blackboard and the degree of opacity of the man standing in front of it.

seems to be transferring between or connecting at least one of the women with the man. In figure 4, the Minolta shows us an audience and some lightwells in a large auditorium while the Kodak shows us the same but with some amazing banners of "something" that looks like slowed-down light streaming out of these lightwells.

Figure 4. Example from the dual camera study: unsensitized camera result (left) and sensitized camera result (right). Note the character of the light emanating from the lightwells in the ceiling.

My working hypothesis concerning this experimental data is that Stan's biofield allowed the sensitized camera to access another level of reality than our normal electric atom/molecule level and to image it on standard Kodak film.

To take this evolving picture to the next level, I need to provide you with some relevant background on key results from our last ten years of psychoenergetics science research:

1. We have discovered a process for imbedding, via a deep meditative state, a specific human intention into a simple electrical device. This device, when switched on in an experimental space (a) conditions that space to a higher electromagnetic (EM) gauge symmetry state than that of our normal electric atom/molecule level of physical reality and (b) tunes that space such that experiments conducted there exhibit material property changes that occur in both the direction of, and close to the magnitude of, the specific intention.

2. Four specific target experiments—using inorganic, organic, and living materials—were designed, run, and evaluated during the years 1997 to 2000. They were all robustly successful.[5]

3. These four experimental outcomes (plus subsequent experiments) have revealed the presence in nature of a second unique level of physical reality that is modulateable by human intention.[6,7]

4. We have also been able to show that the human acupuncture meridian/chakra system is functioning at this same higher EM gauge symmetry level as compared with the rest of the body,

which is functioning at our normal, electric, atom/molecule level.[6] Thus, sustained, directed, human intention can create, in the human biofield, the necessary ingredients to alter the physical properties of our material environment.

5. During the replication phase of one of our target experiments, we learned to devise an experimental measurement system for continuously and quantitatively measuring the degree of thermodynamic free energy change, δG_H^*+, for the aqueous hydrogen ion, H^+, as (a) our "source" device lifts the EM gauge symmetry state of the space or (b) human biofields lift the gauge symmetry state of the space or (c) the lifting occurs in a space that is "information entangled" with (a).[6]

6. The bottom line, here, is that human consciousness is capable of coupling humans and instruments to another unique level of physical reality, not normally detectable by conventional instrumentation, and that this level of reality may have its own set of life-forms, some of which we may be able to image under the appropriate conditions.

Our experiments show that the following equation governs the behavior of a property measurement, Q_M, in a partially conditioned space:

$$Q_M = Q_e + \alpha_{eff} Q_m \qquad (3)$$

Here, α_{eff} is the coupling coefficient between these two levels of physical reality ($0 < \alpha_{eff} < 1$); Q_e is our normal property measurement when $\alpha_{eff} \sim 0$ (just the electric atom/molecule value); and Q_m is the conjugate property measurement value from this second unique level of physical reality (just the magnetic information wave value).

Now we are just one important step away from applying all this to the "orb" phenomenon. Before we can do that, we must come to understand to some degree the phenomenon of macroscopic, room temperature, information entanglement. I do not mean present-day, quantum entanglement, which experimentally is observed only near absolute zero of temperature and for very small objects (molecules, bucky balls, very small crystals, etc.). In this section, I mean information transfer between working laboratories of 1,000 to 10,000 cubic feet size but separated by at least 5,000 to 6,000 miles and with no hard-wired or Internet connection.

To understand our psychoenergetic science experimental results, we have developed a duplex reference frame (RF) for viewing nature's manifold expressions. This RF consists of two, reciprocal, subspaces, one of which is spacetime (x,y,z,t), which we label direct space, or D-space. The other therefore is a frequency domain (k_x, k_y, k_z, k_t) both spatial and temporal, which we label reciprocal space, or R-space. Here, D-space is used as the RF for the subluminal, electric particles, while R-space is used as the RF for the superluminal, magnetic information waves. Together, they form the de Broglie particle/pilot wave concept, which is a key cornerstone for today's formulation of quantum mechanics (QM), and correct the error made by QM's founding fathers, who squeezed both aspects into a space-time formalism.

With minimal coupling ($\propto_{eff}$), de Broglie particle/pilot wave entities exist with $\upsilon_p \upsilon_w = c^2$ (υ_p = electric particle velocity while υ_w =

magnetic information wave velocity). However, there is not enough of the coupler substance left over to allow macroscopic electric materials and macroscopic magnetic information wave materials to be meaningfully coupled, so each isolated macroscopic domain is a U(1) EM gauge symmetry state space.

With substantial coupling ($0 \ll \alpha_{eff} \leq 1$) between the macroscopic substances of the two subspaces, the EM gauge symmetry state of the *combined* binary system is lifted to the higher, SU(2) level and this binary system becomes a higher thermodynamic free energy state where human intention can experimentally influence material properties.

In a state of strong coupling, all parts of an experimental system are substantially connected (entangled) non-locally via R-space. Thus, in our replication experiment of increasing the pH of water in equilibrium with air by +1pH units, via our "Source" (intention) device at four U.S. sites plus their four control sites (no "Source" device) and two European control sites (no "Source" device), our Payson experimental ΔpH results appeared 6,000 miles away within one to three weeks.[6]

What must be understood here is that if we consider a system of sites that are widely separated in D-space, their R-space counterparts must be treated as vectors with both an amplitude, R, and a phase angle, θ, relative to a coordinate direction $\theta = 0$. In R-space, the entire system must be treated as the vector sum of all the parts, and this can be represented by a total system vector, $R_s(k) \exp[i\theta_s(k)]$, where i is the imaginary number $\sqrt{-1}$. However, it is generally the intensity, $I_s(k)$, that one can experimentally measure or perceive, and this is given, for a D-space system consisting of three parts (A,B,C) by

$$I_s(k) = R_s^2(k) = [R_A^2(k) + R_B^2(k) + R_C^2(k)]$$
$$+2\{R_A R_B \cos(\theta_A - \theta_B) + R_A R_C \cos(\theta_A - \theta_C) + R_B R_C \cos(\theta_B - \theta_C)\} \qquad (4)$$

where cos = the cosine function. Here, in equation 4, the [ ] bracket term is what one would have for the R-space system counterpart if there was no interaction between the different parts. The { } bracket term is the sum of the pairwise interactions between the different R-space parts of the overall system.

Thus, recalling equation 3, if $\propto_{eff}$ is significantly greater than zero, our measurement instruments will be able to access Q_m, which is just the integral of $I_s(k)dk$ from zero to some upper value, k^*. To illustrate by using a specific example, consider a typical double-blind medical experiment where A=doctor, B=treatment, and C=placebo. Now we can see that so long as $\propto_{eff} > 0$, combining equations 3 and 4 yields

$$Q_{MB} = Q_{eB} + \propto_{eff} \int_0^{k^*} < R_B^2 + 2\{R_A R_B \cos(\theta_A - \theta_B) + R_{BC} \cos(\theta_B - \theta_C)\} > dk,$$

$$Q_{MC} = Q_{eC} + \propto_{eff} \int_0^{k^*} < R_C^2 + 2\{R_A R_C \cos(\theta_A - \theta_C) + R_{BC} \cos(\theta_B - \theta_C)\} > dk \qquad (5)$$

Although $Q_{eC} \sim 0$ while Q_{eB} is not, if $\propto$eff is sufficiently large and the phase angle differences are appropriate, Q_{MC} may approach Q_{MB} in magnitude and clinical trials could fail because the placebo effect is so large.

On a slightly different tack, Enserink wrote a short article in *Science* magazine (1999) noting that, in the early 1980s, double-blind, obsessive-compulsive disorder experiments showed the placebo-response to be very small (less than 15 percent) compared to the treatment effect.[7] However, in 1999, a meta-analysis of nineteen antidepressant drug trials showed an average placebo effect of 75 percent compared to the *real* drug effect. Perhaps the most important question one should ask here is why the magnitude of the placebo effect has increased so remarkably in the past twenty years. One could add to this for the same time period (a) cosmological observations regarding outward acceleration of the Universe at its outer edges and (b) cosmological observations concerning the presence of both dark energy and dark matter abundance in nature.

My present working hypothesis regarding this experimental data is that the concentration of active "coupler" substance in the cosmos, and certainly in our local Universe, has been slowly increasing for many decades. If so, $\propto_{eff}$ would be growing in magnitude. This would allow the placebo effect to approximate the treatment effect in double-blind, placebo experiments; it would herald the end of useful double-blind experiments; it would rationalize why the degree of "connectivity" between humans seems to be increasing with time and why, on the average, we might be experiencing "orbs" with our digital cameras at this time.

All of the foregoing experimental data indicates a profound connectivity between any one part of nature and another. Every one of us can influence all biological life-forms around us via our biofield emissions and the information that they carry, whether we intend to or not. Figure 5 provides a simple picture of the general *system* of interactive elements involved in *any* communication event, whether we be a minister, a healer, a medical doctor, a acupuncturist, a teacher, a performer, a spouse, a parent, or a photographer of orbs. In all cases, equations 3 to 5 are involved.

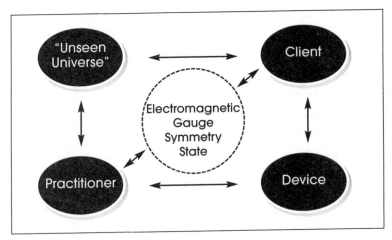

Figure 5. The five key elements that may be participating interactively and influencing any human communication.

For our interest in this foreword, make the following substitutions: *experimenter* for *practitioner*, *camera* for *device*, and *orbs* for *client*. If the experimenter's biofield is strong enough to "condition" the space and the camera, and if the orbs are a life-form of the R-space domain, *they should be photographable* provided certain technical conditions hold. This could occur if they are sufficiently information entangled with us. The orbs are certainly not creatures of our spacetime world. This type of photographic evidence should be accessible with even higher-dimensional life-forms under the appropriate circumstances.

—William A. Tiller, Ph.D.
Professor Emeritus, Stanford University

Notes

1. Irvin Rock, *The Nature of Perceptual Adaptation* (New York: Basic Books, 1966).

2. Stewart Wolf, *Educating Doctors* (New Brunswick, N.J.: Transaction Publishers, 1997).

3. Glen Rein and Rollin McCraty, "Local and Non-Local Effects of Coherent Heart Frequencies on Conformational Changes of DNA," *Proceedings of the Joint USPA/IAPR Psychotronics Conference,* Milwaukee, Wisc., 1993.

4. W. A. Tiller, *Science and Human Transformation* (Walnut Creek, Calif.: Pavior Publishing, 1997).

5. W. A. Tiller, W. E. Dibble, Jr., and M. J. Kohane, *Conscious Acts of Creation* (Walnut Creek, Calif.: Pavior Publishing, 2001).

6. W. A. Tiller, W. E. Dibble, Jr., and J. G. Fandel, *Some Science Adventures with Real Magic* (Walnut Creek, Calif: Pavior Publishing, 2005).

7. Martin Enserink, "Can the Placebo Be the Cure?" *Science* 284 (9 April 1999): 238–40.

Preface

In the past decade, photographers all over the world have been witnesses to a curious phenomenon. As digital cameras began to replace conventional film cameras, circular-shaped optical anomalies were reported to appear in photographs taken all over the world, in all sorts of conditions. Even more unusual, these anomalies had not been visible to the naked eye at the time the pictures were taken, and no physical objects or matter could be identified that might have caused them. People wondered: Could these features be energy fields beyond the range of human sight, connected with realities that are outside of normal human perception? The phenomenon aroused considerable interest, and the types of explanations put forward to explain them were legion.

The initial reaction was—predictably—to classify them as spirits, or disincarnate entities of some type, so that the orbs were grouped with ghosts and became the focus of much attention from groups that called themselves "ghost hunters."

Others scoffed at the idea and put considerable effort into proving that orb images can be explained away by various forms of pollution in the atmosphere or by certain anomalies in camera mechanisms.

At present, there is little published literature of a serious kind on orbs, while there is abundant information on the Internet that reflects the wide-ranging explanations that people have put forth to explain the phenomenon.

When Cynthia Black, the editor in chief of Beyond Words Publishing, first approached us with the suggestion of publishing our separate work on orbs together in one book, we were both intrigued but somewhat concerned about how such a joint venture could work. But after reading each other's manuscripts, our concerns faded away and our interest kept growing.

For decades, both of us had been on similar paths. Míceál, who served as a Catholic theologian for more than thirty-five years, had been pursuing research into spirituality and Jesus. He had started studying orbs with great passion in 2001, two years before Klaus did. Klaus, an experimental physicist with relentless interest in spirituality and the nature of the spiritual reality, had long since found traditional Christian fundamentalism too confining when he experienced his first encounter with orbs. Míceál, the theologian, immediately sensed that investigating the phenomenon of orbs would constitute a major milestone in terms of scientific insight into a multilayered spiritual realm with physical ramifications. And Klaus, the physicist, immediately suspected that the photography of orbs would turn into a significant piece of the puzzle toward proof that the Spiritual reality at large is for real.

We had thus both bravely crossed the lines of our academic expertise and ended in presenting a classical example of synergism: the combined results of our individual paths. Discovering the nature and significance of orbs clearly surpasses the sum of the orbs' components. Orbs cast a new light on the philosophical/spiritual/scientific realization that "All is One." In this expanded way of looking at reality, our diverse findings are fundamentally congruent. The presentation of our views and findings in this separate format allows you, the reader, to experience firsthand this synergism of the theological/scientific and scientific/theological frames.

Convinced that the phenomenon offered us a valuable tool by which we could obtain a richer perspective on the nature of reality—if we could avoid the two extremes of profound skepticism and enthusiastic credulity—we decided to collaborate on a book, each of us presenting our own unique record of findings and interpretations. Our fields of expertise, our experimental approach, and our conclusions complement each other superbly for a study of this kind.

The material presented here is the result of several years of careful, entirely independent research of the orb phenomenon by two authors who had not known each other and who were unaware of each other's work prior to the publisher's initiative for this collaboration. We offer it to those of open mind who may wish to investigate these matters for themselves. We describe how our involvement with this work began and the mistakes and pitfalls that we encountered in a way that will provide a great service to those who may wish to study orbs themselves, while offering tantalizing suggestions and insights on what the implications of the orb phenomenon may be for our understanding of reality.

Mícéal Ledwith, D.D., LL.D.
Klaus Heinemann, Ph.D.

Part I

The Orb
Phenomenon

by
Míceál Ledwith, D.D., LL.D.

Foreword to Part I

All my life, I have seen wonderful things that were very normal to me but were certainly not to anyone else. During my childhood in Texas, my mother picked cotton for just pennies a pound. Our home had no running water or electricity, no furniture, no wallpaper, no art, no yard with flowers—just bare ground and alfalfa. We were dirt poor. Without money for doctors or medicine, my mother used her innate abilities to heal sick family members, see omens and visions, and have prophetic dreams. These remarkable abilities guided her daily life. I was blessed because those harsh circumstances—this stark environment, the absence of basic material necessities—made me find within myself the marvelous, uncommon abilities unused by most people. As Shakespeare wrote, "Sweet are the uses of Adversity."

Among the wonderful experiences I had was a profound love of God and an understanding of what that love really was. Later in my life I went to church and tried to understand God and creation from the point of view of religious doctrine. But it was in conflict not only with what I felt but with what I knew.

Then, thirty years ago, I began a dramatic new life phase that made perfect sense of all the experiences of my youth. The entity Ramtha entered my life and began speaking through me. Early on in our relationship he taught me how to transcend my physical reality. To be more accurate, he actually yanked me out of my body. I found myself flying through a shining, rotating tunnel filled with the sounds of rushing winds—the music into the next level of reality. Eventually

I hit what looked like a white wall and returned to my body. What seemed like ten minutes had really been more like six hours. After this experience and many others like it, I was left with the challenge of explaining to people how it was possible to be endowed with a divine mind and yet be separate from it.

Over the years I have seen things in those encounters that I suppose other people could hardly imagine in their wildest dreams. I have seen other universes, have watched life come and go, and have met extraordinary beings in other dimensions. I've seen the other side of that grand illusion called death.

Ramtha has always challenged those who take part in his teachings to apply them in the light of scientific knowledge, practical experiment, and everyday life. In that way we no longer need to believe; we know. The subject of orbs is a case in point. Ramtha had spoken of beings who inhabit other planes of existence. I had seen those beings myself, but I had to keep it to myself because people so often become fanatical about "the supernatural." Five or six years ago Ramtha gave a long set of teachings on what he called the "orb entities." I had many experiences with them, as I wrote in my autobiography, *A State of Mind*. Not only did I see these balls of light, but they often *chose* the books for me to read and would congregate so densely over *their* pages of interest that I tried to wipe them off the page so I could read what all of the hubbub was about! They are not just a ball of curious light but rather what you and I are *out of our bodies!* We are the Ball of Light that is the life-force of our brain and body.

After Ramtha introduced me to orbs, I began to see them faintly recorded on the early digital photographs we took. This remains a delightful experience for me—to see what I had held secret for so long becoming manifested at large. Since then multitudes of these orb beings have been participants and observers at every event at the Ramtha School.

Míceál Ledwith was one of those who embarked on a remarkable and detailed long-term study of the orb beings at that time Ramtha taught about them. He now has more than one hundred thousand orb images in his collection. In this book he describes his remarkable experiences on this journey and explains the best circumstances for detecting orbs. He draws from that many intriguing conclusions, not only about what the orbs are in themselves but also the implications they have for so many of our cherished fundamental beliefs that now, as he says, "stand in sore need of redefinition."

—JZ Knight

Introduction

"There Are More Things in Heaven and on Earth. . . ."

People have always been fascinated by the paranormal, whether that takes the form of revulsion, keen interest, or morbid dread. Whenever I look back at what historical sources we have on this subject, I am always struck by how remarkably consistent the content of the paranormal has remained—across all cultures—right to the present day: ghosts, poltergeist activity, hauntings, angels, goblins, unexplained phenomena, precognition, prophecies, séances, demons, and ectoplasm. In many ways it is this collection of phenomena, rather than any other fact, that has been the major influence in defining how we think of the realms of "the beyond." One can't help but notice how many events that were once perceived as paranormal lie at the roots of almost all religion. Paranormal experiences, particularly ghosts, poltergeist activity, and precognitive phenomena, encouraged humans to believe that there was something greater than our frailty, which helped assuage our need to know how we fit in to the scheme of things, and above all assured us that everything we are is not irretrievably lost at death.

But recently the gallery of the paranormal has acquired a new and radically different kind of addition from what I have described above, especially since point-and-shoot digital cameras have become common. Mysterious objects, of a spherical or circular shape, which were not visible to the naked eye, began to appear in pictures taken in all sorts of situations. Like many a new arrival on any scene, these entities are unpredictable and irreverent and don't always oblige by obeying our traditionally accepted rules. In fact, they often seem to behave like the adolescents of the paranormal world, bringing chaos to the tidy, stuffy structures we knew in the past. Or maybe they seem to behave this way simply because it's the first time that we have encountered the paranormal in a readily accessible form, easily available for observation by anyone on a regular basis, almost at will.

The advent of digital cameras, of course, did not mark the beginning of this phenomenon, which came to be known as *orbs*. I myself have some examples of pictures of these mysterious shapes I took as far back as the early 1990s with an ordinary film camera. However, there is no doubt that the coming of the digital camera made a major difference in the circumstances and frequency with which this phenomenon was photographed all over the world by people of every age, race, color, creed, or class.

Unlike many other "paranormal" experiences, the orb phenomenon is fortunately not the preserve of experts or gurus, or of those who believe they are specially favored in some way by God. The orb realities can be experienced and evaluated repeatedly by anyone. For a period of five or six years before being asked to put this book together, I had been taking great numbers of photographs of these mysterious energy forms on a daily basis. At the time of this writing I have a collection that numbers well in excess of one hundred thousand orb images, and I know of several other large collections. Every person who has a simple digital or even a film camera, and some time and patience, can do the same. They can then evaluate their own pictures, without having to take any "expert's" word for anything.

Fortunately we live in a skeptical age when delusions and illusions are not welcomed as avidly as they once were. That may help to put a brake on our instinctive tendency to lump any new phenomenon into the nearest category with which we are familiar. But to regard orbs superficially as just ghosts, evil spirits, or spirits of the dead would be unfortunate; for assuredly, whatever we may come to know of them, they are far more than that. Realities of a kind that we never believed existed are probably what we are looking at in the orb phenomenon.

It is also regrettable that so much of the discussion around the orb phenomenon has occurred in the investigation of the "paranormal" and the "supernatural" or in the examination of places that have a reputation for being haunted. Many researchers of the paranormal have risked life and limb to go to damp graveyards and allegedly haunted locations, in inaccessible parts of the countryside, in the dead of night. They could have conducted perhaps even better research from the comfort of their own front porches, while significantly reducing the risk of pneumonia. Our culture and history have slotted these phenomena into the categories of "ghostly" and "occult," but we will do much better in these investigations—and be much less frightened, cold, and damp in the process—if we remember that orbs and the realms they inhabit are fundamentally not a matter of faith but of physics.

However, a new kind of prejudice that may impede fairness of treatment for the orb phenomenon has recently come our way. According to a 1998 study in the journal *Nature* that asked members of the National Academy of Sciences about their spiritual beliefs, about

72 percent expressed disbelief in the existence of a personal god. Many of our leading scientific thinkers, turned off by secondhand mythologies about a secondhand God that have nothing to do with the real thing, have concluded that there is no such thing as survival of the death of the physical body or any form of existence except the physical version we know. When a large portion of the people in the vanguard of creative thought and discovery do not believe in any spiritual reality, human beings are the real losers in the bleak landscape of atheism, and close in their wake come the orbs; if people do not believe in any spiritual reality, they are unlikely to believe that orbs are spirits from another dimension.

In many ways it reminds me of the famous case of the Viennese obstetrician Dr. Ignaz Semmelweis. In 1861 he showed conclusively that there was a connection between the many fatalities due to childbirth fever and physicians not washing their hands between conducting autopsies and delivering babies. Since the technology to detect germs did not exist at that time, most mainstream physicians ridiculed him for proposing that there were invisible agents of potentially fatal diseases.

Nothing can substitute for a rigorous scientific attitude in any investigation. But a contemptuous attitude toward anything that will not readily fit into a test tube, pot, or pan does not meet the qualifications of rigor, objectivity, and open-mindedness required for the scientific study of any subject. I am hopeful that the study of orbs will not be lumped in uncritically with the tradition of the paranormal where they do not belong. If they were to be so relegated, a fascinating area of discovery would suffer significant damage. I am also hopeful that this new study would not continue to be dismissed uncritically by those who would nevertheless claim to have objective and scientific minds.

Put off by religions' feeble attempts to explain what lies beyond death, and by the absence of any attempt, feeble or otherwise, to say what precedes life, this category of people seems to be totally skeptical of anything that might provide evidence of what lies beyond the everyday world that we know through the senses. These individuals maintain, for example, that all orb pictures can be explained away as due to moisture particles, spots on the lens, dust or pollen particles rising from the unpaved roads or grass we have just walked over, stains coming from film processing, flaws in digital camera technology, optical lens flares, or *bokeh* (a Japanese word meaning "blur," referring to a picture's out-of-focus areas). Most of the published literature is neither friendly nor scientific.

An exception is a rigorous investigation from 2005 conducted by Gary E. Schwartz and Katherine Creath of the University of Arizona.[1] Based on a small selection of orb pictures, this paper correctly warns against too readily attributing orb phenomena in digital photographs to some form of paranormal agency and investigates how stray reflections in uncontrolled environments might produce results such as these. However, the authors also acknowledge that it would be neither logical nor responsible at this stage to dismiss all orb phenomena as due to mechanisms such as stray reflections. Had the authors access to better data—such as is presented in this book—rather than their limited selection of images, it would be interesting to know their assessment.

1. Gary E. Schwartz and Katherine Creath, "Anomalous Orbic 'Spirit' Photographs? A Conventional Optic Explanation," *Journal of Scientific Exploration* 19, no. 3 (2005): 343–58.

There is no doubt that dust particles, pollen, or moisture droplets in the air can produce images that may in some respects resemble true orb photographs, and care must be taken to assess the evidence. It is likewise true that some camera mechanisms in certain circumstances will produce false pictures of orbs. But it takes very little experience to be able to clearly distinguish the false from the real. (I offer guidance for doing so in chapter 6.) Nor do we have before us just ten or twenty blurred pictures that claim to have captured something of the miraculous or supernatural. The small selection of my own photographs that I have included in this book comes from more than one hundred thousand such pictures that I have taken over the past five or six years, and I know of many other large collections. These pictures were selected not on the basis of being the most vivid or dramatic in my collection but for what new insights they could provide in the study of this field.

The orb phenomenon poses an entirely new question for us, and this I believe to be the main area of interest. Do dimensions exist altogether beyond the material ones we know, and what would the implications of that be for how we understand ourselves? Just four hundred years ago Giordano Bruno was burned to death in Rome by the Inquisition for suggesting there might be intelligent life outside this earth. In terms of affront to diehard orthodoxy, religious or secular, the emergence of this new question may well turn Giordano Bruno's offence into a peccadillo. For indeed it does seem that we have never yet fully realized the import of Shakespeare's famous dictum, "There are more things in heaven and earth . . . than are dreamt of in your philosophy." The orb phenomenon may turn out to be one of the most remarkable things we have met so far, not just for what it may be in itself, but more important, for what light it might shed on the human race's attempts to understand itself and where it fits into the cosmos. It may have devastating implications for the traditional ways in which we picture many central religious beliefs, including our understanding of the "beyond." But it can teach us an enormous amount about the nature of reality beyond what we call "this world" and what we need to realize about ourselves and our world to fit into that new framework of understanding.

A Photographic
Journey of Discovery

I first read about orbs in JZ Knight's autobiography, *A State of Mind*, describing events that took place in the late 1970s.[1] She told of little globes of different colored light whose activity on the pages of the book she was reading would go frantic when she came across something of great significance. I later heard a long and detailed discourse about orbs during a series of remarkable teachings given by Ramtha during 2001 and 2002. I soon discovered that Ramtha had first taught about orbs more than twenty years before that, in the early 1980s, and that orb photography has been commonplace at every event held at the Ramtha School for more than five years.[2]

---

1. JZ Knight, *A State of Mind: My Story: Ramtha, the Adventure Begins* (New York: Warner Brothers, 1987), 359.

2. Ramtha, the Enlightened One, channeled by JZ Knight, *Ramtha: The White Book*, edited by Steven Lee Weinberg (Yelm, Wash.: JZK Publishing, revised and expanded edition, 2004), 89, 203.

Inspired by Ramtha's vast body of information, I began to photograph orbs in a systematic way. I was still at that stage not quite sure of the precise nature of the orbs or where exactly they fit into the conventional range of the paranormal. Consequently I began by photographing them at the same time every night on my property (all but two of the pictures in part 1 of this book were taken on my property), since the night is what the "ghostly" has always been associated with.

Some of my friends didn't help matters by telling me they wouldn't like to have this phenomena around *their* houses. I responded by saying at least it was always done in a relatively safe, secure, and unscary place, right outside my own front door! However, I soon discovered that if I had a dark background I could just as successfully take orb photographs at high noon, since the orbs apparently had no preference. By the end of the first year I had amassed a collection of nearly fifteen thousand orb images, and usually I was taking between one hundred and two hundred images per day in the latter part of the year.

The First Breakthrough:
The More You Photograph, the More Orbs Appear

Orbs are a fascinating subject for photography and became more so to me with the variety of forms that started to appear after months of my sustained focus on them. I believed that, as with any subject, I could learn more and more about them by continued study.

The first breakthrough that I had occurred only a few months after I started taking the photographs. In the first ten pictures or so that I shot each night, few if any orbs were present, and I found this very curious.

As time passed, and more and more pictures were taken, the number of orbs appearing in the photos began to increase quite remarkably.

I told this fact to several other people who also were interested in investigating orbs. Some of them suggested that the orbs were being attracted to us because of our focus and interest in them. While I was ready to accept that explanation I also believed that there were more prosaic explanations that needed to be considered as well: If I opted only for the obvious and appealing explanation that the orbs were pleased with our attention, I could miss some vital piece of tangible physical evidence that might open the way to a much deeper understanding of the orbs and how they might fit in with what we knew. Ramtha had taught us what this phenomenon was; through my investigation, I could learn more of its detail and its implications for our own understanding of reality.

The really interesting orb photographs only began to appear after I had spent one or two hours each day in actual photography or computer analysis of the images. If I kept up that pattern consistently over a number of days, the results were usually quite dramatic; if I did not, the results were rarely notable. In short, I realized that orb photography is not something that can be done satisfactorily by rushing out to snap a few pictures during commercial breaks in your favorite soap operas. Later in this book I will describe what physical processes may account for this greater number of orbs.

The Second Breakthrough: Hexagonal-shaped Orbs

During this time of intense focus and effort something very interesting started to occur. I had been photographing the same group of orbs consistently for about ten days and in the same location near my house in late October 2002. One night, in several photographs, the orbs did not come out in their usual spherical shape, but as hexagons (shapes with six angles and six sides) of a very striking form. This did not occur all of the time—maybe once in every five pictures. Only the orbs were affected in the pictures; everything else appeared as normal. (See figures I-1 and I-2 in the color section for examples of these hexagonal orbs.)

I did not know what to make of this phenomenon at first. Then I came to realize that the orbs' hexagonal shape reminded me of the shape formed by the "leaves" that make up the digital camera shutter when they are opening and closing the lens. Cameras can have a shutter made up of one piece or "leaf," but it is normal today to have a shutter made up of two to six leaves. A six-sided shutter will give a six-sided shape to the lens opening.

The more components or leaves, the closer to a circle the opening becomes, and a circle is of course the optimum shape for a lens opening to produce good-quality, focused images. In this way the shutter functions like the iris of the human eye. I came to suspect that the resemblance between the hexagonal shape of the orbs in the pictures and the shape of the aperture that a six-leaf camera shutter makes when opening and closing might not be accidental. I also noted that the orbs assumed shapes of the same patterns no matter which way the camera was held: right way up, sideways, or upside down.

Suppose in our first picture the bottom third was sliced off the orb. If I now turn the camera upside down and take a second picture, I find it is the top third of the orb that has been sliced off. This can only mean that the orb images merely reflect the lens shape. I began to ponder what could cause this camera shutter pattern to be imprinted on the orbs in the picture.

In digital photography, if the camera is moved while a picture is being taken, especially in dim light conditions, you can easily get a double image. For example, suppose you are taking a picture of someone standing in front of a plain wall, and while doing so you point the camera at an adjacent wall where there is a doorway. If the shutter remains open while you point the camera at the second background, then the camera will record a double image—the original scene with the person standing against a plain wall superimposed over the image of the wall with the doorway in it.

We now actually have two independent but rather faint images. Because neither received sufficient light to properly record it, the image as a whole seems ghostly. We have all seen ghostly or transparent people in such images. They are not evidence of the paranormal but of poor technique. That being said, genuine images of transparency have also been recorded.

The Third Breakthrough: Light Source

I wondered if some form of this double imaging was occurring to produce the sort of hexagonal pattern I was getting on some of the orbs. I suspected that there must be more than one light source operating for the camera to be able to record such images. At first I thought the flash was emitting two bursts of light, such as many cameras do today, but that would affect everything in the picture, not just the shape of the orbs.

After several weeks spent trying to understand this phenomenon it suddenly dawned on me that the only way this could occur would be if the second light source was coming from within the orbs themselves. This second light source was recording the image of the orbs on the camera, whereas the remainder of the scene—trees, cars, people, and houses—was being recorded by the other light source: the camera flash being reflected back into the lens.

But what could cause the orbs to emit a light back from within themselves?

At this point I realized I needed to investigate a puzzling fact: The camera flash seemed to be *almost* essential to successfully taking orb pictures, even in broad daylight.

The Role of the Flash

The average duration of a camera flash is about one one-thousandth of a second. I had thought at the beginning of my observations that the flash's speed is what made it possible to capture orb images; I presumed that the orbs existed in a much higher frequency state than ours and that their movements might be too fast to be captured by the shutter speed alone. Even though I was by then also taking photographs of orbs in broad daylight and had seen the orbs myself without either a camera or flash, the best results were obtained when I used a flash.

I soon abandoned the theory that the flash's speed was what made capturing the orbs in pictures possible, because it made no sense. The advantage of a flash is that it can "freeze" a picture of a rapidly moving object. It gives an image of how it was, in that precise millisecond of the flash, without blurring, even though the shutter speed (the length of time the aperture remains open during the taking of a photograph) might not in itself be rapid enough to "freeze" the motion of the object.

But if objects are moving too fast for the shutter to capture the images of the orbs without blurring, the camera will still capture an image of the fast-moving object, however blurred it may be. It was obvious therefore that the flash's speed could have nothing to do with capturing a very high speed or high frequency object like an orb; pictures of them, even if blurred, should still occur when no flash was used. But this usually did not happen.

As I explained earlier, it became obvious to me that there was an unmistakable connection between the hexagonal shapes the spherical orbs had assumed in many of my pictures and the hexagonal pattern of a six-leaf camera shutter. It seemed to me that the images were being formed on the camera's CCD (charge-coupled device)[3] when the shutter was partly open, whereas to capture a proper picture the shutter would have to be fully open. The partially open shutter was obviously cropping the orb shapes.

I soon realized that somehow the light from the orbs was not getting to the camera while the shutter was still fully open for that fraction of a second. Yet even if this were so, it was still difficult to understand why only the orbs were changed into hexagonal shapes and everything else in the picture appeared normal. Another piece of the puzzle was needed to explain this.

3. A CCD is the sensitive plate that records the images, like film in a conventional camera.

If the orbs were being recorded photographically in the same way as everything else then this shape change would not occur. There had to be some difference in the way the orb was captured by the camera and the way in which the remainder of the picture was captured. Normally photographic images are formed when the light from the flash reflects off the objects back to the camera. This did not seem to be the case with the orbs. The only explanation I could come up with was that the orbs must have been generating the light that made them visible *from within themselves*. There had to be some process that caused this, and I theorized that the light from the camera flash must in some way trigger it. This is what led me to believe that the only conceivable explanation of the hexagonal shapes (or half moon, or triangular shapes) was that the camera was recording *not* the flash reflected back from the orbs but rather a light that came from within the orbs themselves.

This led me to consider another phenomenon that could help explain how the light was being produced: ionization.

A Clue from Ionization

Every orb photographer is aware that during rain or high humidity far more orbs are present than is the case in dry conditions. One factor that could cause this is that the atmosphere's electrons are excited by rainfall. Elsewhere in this book I explain how difficult it is to confuse photographs of raindrops with genuine orb pictures. Nevertheless, it is important for the orb photographer to understand what processes are involved in association with rainfall, as this is one of the most controversial areas of orb photography.

Ionization occurs when electrons are propelled from one atomic shell to another. The atmosphere's nitrogen and oxygen gases have two atoms each, which are held together by a sharing of their orbiting electrons. Unless these electrons are hit by a photon or energy particle they remain in their basic energy state. Above the basic state are many empty energy levels (or shelves). When a photon or energy particle that has enough power hits an electron, the electron is forced up and perhaps beyond the vacant energy shelf, right outside of the two-atom molecules. The electron is now free of its original molecule, and that molecule becomes a positive ion. If the freed electron attaches to a neutral molecule it becomes a negative ion. If the electron attaches to a positive ion, it normally lodges in one of the vacant energy shelves and gives off a photon equal in energy to the energy given up by the formerly free electron.

The electron's frequency determines the frequency and color of the photon, so now we begin to see the extraordinary fact that *it is possible for the atmosphere's molecules to radiate in any color of the light spectrum!* The energy of light photons is measured in electron volts. For example, energy of less than 1.65 electron volts will give off a photon of infrared color radiation. Energy of more than 3.26 electron volts will give off a photon radiating at the ultraviolet level.

Rainfall generates free electrons that can bombard the atmosphere's atoms, or possibly the atoms of the orbs themselves, and cause ionization. If ionization occurs in the orbs themselves, it helps the orbs begin a process known in physics as *fluorescence* (fluorescence, which will be described in chapter 2, is when a molecule absorbs light of one energy and later emits light of a lower energy); photons will be generated from within the orbs and thus become recorded on the camera CCD, or even be visible to the naked eye in certain conditions.

So what we are observing in the orb photographs might not be the orb beings themselves but the ionizing effect their energy has on the surrounding atmosphere.

Whatever explanation may be valid, it would be a mistake to say that no legitimate researcher takes photographs in any form of precipitation. In fact, if care is taken to ensure the effects of the raindrops are not confused with orbs, during precipitation may be one of the most rewarding times of all in which to conduct investigations. Despite that I must point out that most of the photographs I have included in this book were *not* taken during rainfall.

The Plot Thickens: Communication?

I had begun to suspect that the taking on of the hexagonal shape might not be an entirely random thing. Weeks could pass before the hexagonal shapes appeared again; and even when they did they did not feature in every photograph, which is what would be more likely if it were due only to a camera malfunction.

At that point in my experimentation, the phenomenon happened only when photographing those particular orbs in my backyard. Given that these apparent camera malfunctions seemed to follow no obvious patterns or logic I began to wonder if it was possible that they were actually being effected in some way by the orbs themselves. Needless to say, this was not a possibility that I had been expecting or had been very open to. If the orbs were electromagnetic in nature, then it was entirely plausible for them to be able to cause such an electromagnetic phenomenon, which amounted only to milliseconds of difference in timing between flash and shutter. In fact, an electromagnetic signal might be the most obvious first form of communication to be attempted—that is, if the orbs were interested or capable of some form of communication.

This at first seemed to me to be an outlandish explanation indeed, and I anticipate most of my readers will think the same. But I decided to test out this theory. I formulated questions, after which I would take a photograph to see what form the orbs would take as a response to the question. I decided that we would let the hexagon form stand for a "yes" reply to a question, and the ordinary spherical form, presumably being easier to manifest, would stand for a "no" response. I tested this out by asking questions with obvious answers, and from that time on there followed a lengthy period of communication. It was necessary to wait about thirty seconds for a response to come, and if I rushed the process there was no alteration in the orb form.

Over the course of several weeks, through this slow and tedious process I posed a long list of questions. At the end of that period these particular orbs did not appear anymore, nor have they appeared since. Subsequently the camera functioned normally: no further hexagonal-shaped orb images were obtained.

Before we move on to orb coloring, let me summarize this chapter's findings. I discovered early on that capturing orbs in photographs is much more successful if the photography has continued for some time. The appearance of hexagonal-shaped orb images gave me the first clue that the orbs register not through the reflected light from the flash but from a light emerging from within the orbs themselves. This fluoresced light reaches the camera lens shortly after the reflected light from the flash. This means it is best to use a flash when photographing orbs, even in broad daylight, as it is the flash that sparks the fluorescence that makes them visible to the camera. Ionization of the atmosphere is also a great help in gaining good orb pictures because the amount of free electrons generated helps the fluorescence process. The delay in the light emanating from within the orbs themselves being registered by the camera is what formed the basis of the communication I established by allowing the hexagonal- and spherical-shaped orb pictures to stand for a "yes" and "no" response respectively.

2

The Significance
of Orb Coloring

O ne of the most surprising and beautiful sights to behold at the beginning of orb photography is the wide range of colors the orbs exhibit: normally shades of red, white, blue, green, gold, and rose. Beautiful though this is, orb coloring also provides us with significant clues about their nature.

We are well aware that human faculties such as hearing and sight operate in a very narrow band and that the hearing and seeing abilities of most animals leave our capabilities in the dust. But modest though our power of sight undoubtedly is, it has an even greater limitation: Human vision operates only within a limited range of the electromagnetic spectrum. Knowing this, it is actually comical to ponder how readily anything that falls outside that narrow band is dismissed as unreal or regarded with some mixture of fear or wonder. A good example is the way we think of ghosts.

Isaac Newton gave our range of colors the Latin term *spectrum*, which means "a showing forth," "an apparition," or "an appearance." All electromagnetic radiation is characterized by its frequency (wavelength) and by the strength of its radiation (intensity). The human eye is able to detect electromagnetic radiation in the range of about 380 to 780 nanometers (nm, one-billionth of a meter). This range constitutes what we call the visible spectrum and is known in physics as "visible light"—basically the range covered by the colors of the rainbow.

The Wacky World of Quantum Physics

Obviously orbs fall well outside of this range because they are rarely, if ever, visible to the naked eye. But to understand them better we need to look at a few more strange facts about the realms of reality we inhabit. Several Nobel Prize–winning physicists have posited that the "physical" world is in fact one vast sea of energy, that nothing is really solid but is mostly composed of empty space. What is even stranger is that apparently it all continually flashes in and out of existence in a fraction of a second. It appears to us as solid only because we vibrate at the same frequency and because we flash in and out of existence in perfect concert with the physical environment. Our thoughts coagulate this fluid sea of energy into what we perceive as "objects."

Welcome to the world of quantum physics.

The levels of reality above this "physical" world seem to us to be even less solid than this, but presumably that is only because their frequency is different. We tend to see "this" world as real, and everything else is just levels of "frequencies." Now we have to wonder whether we can show that those frequencies are actually realms that are just as substantial as this "physical" one, as Ramtha taught. To a being "above" our physical realm perhaps our reassuringly solid Earth appears quite ghostly and insubstantial.

The closest frequency realm to our physical world is infrared, which has a wavelength of about 1,000 nm and an electron voltage of about 1.24. This is well beyond the range of wavelength that a human person normally can see, but it is the realm in which orbs first appear. By comparison, far-ultraviolet has a wavelength of only about 200 nm and the very high electron voltage of about 6.20.

Now you may wonder what all of this has to do with understanding orbs. *It has everything to do with it,* and in fact it opens the door to one of the most valuable clues readily available to us in trying to decide what the orbs really are.

How we divide colors from one another is largely a matter of taste and the terms we have customarily used. The actual perception of color is of course a vast topic in the science of optics, which falls far outside the range of this book. However, there are some simple aspects of optics that will be very helpful for us to contemplate here.

Are We Seeing Colors That Are Outside the Visible Spectrum?

The colors the digital camera perceives in the orbs, though undoubtedly colors of the visible spectrum, apparently are not actually being perceived by the camera within the visible spectrum. If they were, then everybody would see them with the naked eye all the time. So what is the digital camera actually "seeing"? How does it register these colors that are invisible to the human eye?

The obvious and simple answer of course is to say that when the digital camera picks up infrared light, there is no way it can be shown as such on the little screen on the back of your camera, nor can it be printed on photographic paper. The camera is designed to convert invisible low-infrared light into a form of light and color that *is* visible to human beings, or else digital camera sales would take a nosedive! So we are not seeing low infrared light on our camera screens, even though the orbs are emitting low infrared light. We are seeing infrared light converted into an adjacent lower frequency to make it visible to us.

But the matter is not quite so simple, for we can on occasion also see orbs with the naked eye. It is doubtful that our eyes and brains are converting the hitherto invisible infrared light and beyond into a form of light that we can see. Rather, it seems more likely that we are seeing what is actually there, and we are seeing it outside of the visible light spectrum. The problem, or clue (if we prefer to see it more positively), is that we have been told those colors exist only in the wavelength and frequencies of "visible light." Yet now we can see that they might possibly exist *outside* that spectrum range.

So is it that the range of colors in the visible light spectrum may also exist beyond that spectrum in equivalent forms but are only visible to us when we are in certain states of consciousness? If this is true, then each realm of frequency that lies "above" us may perhaps replicate, or echo, the range of colors that make up the visible light spectrum but in a much more intense and vibrant harmonic form. Furthermore, if this is true, then what the digital camera is picking up in the low infrared range may not be invisible light that is being converted into a visible light form by the camera for our viewing pleasure but may in fact be some form of harmonic version—or echo, if you will—in the invisible infrared plane of the colors that are familiar to us from the visible light spectrum.

We now have at least some interesting hypotheses about the "beyond": First, these bands of frequencies above us might actually be realms of existence that would be as solid to the entities that may inhabit them as our world is to us. Second, harmonics of the visible light spectrum might possibly also exist as colors in those realms. I will discuss the optimum conditions for orb photography in relation to these two hypotheses in a later section.

As the result of years of investigation, I must here add a third postulate, which could also radically alter our understanding of reality. I have no doubt that, regardless of atmospheric conditions, the orbs can affect the time and circumstances in which they can be detected. On many occasions, the first picture I take contains no orbs; then, just ten seconds later, my picture of the sky is filled with orbs. And in the third picture, taken ten seconds later still, almost no orbs are present. If several people with identical cameras take the same pictures at the same time, some will get a lot of orbs, others few or none at all. The overwhelming nature of this evidence has to show at least a significant level of consciousness in most if not all of the orb forms. It is equally evident that they can also exhibit a group "mind" when they appear, disappear, or otherwise maneuver in perfect unity—much as a huge flock of birds swoops and banks as one entity against an evening sky.

Orbs and Our Perception of Color

This is a complex topic in optics, but it can be summarized simply for our purposes here as it is an important consideration in understanding orbs.

Broadly speaking, an object can react with light in three different ways.

- It can totally absorb the light that is cast on it, and reflect nothing back, in which case the object will appear black. This is called *absorption*.
- If the object reflects back all the wavelengths of the light that is shone on it, it will appear white. This is termed *reflection*.
- If the object has a rough rather than a smooth surface, it will scatter the different wavelengths of light from its surface with different degrees of success. This is termed *scattering*, and it is a combination of the first two. The human eye will perceive the scattering object as having the color or combination of colors that corresponds to the wavelengths of the light the object reflects best.[1]

---

1. I am obviously leaving out of consideration here objects that emit light due to some internal chemical reaction, or that are iridescent because they are at a sufficiently high temperature themselves to generate light from within. Likewise, it is clear to anyone who has spent time photographing orbs that a significant proportion of orbs are translucent or transparent, at least in part. Transparent objects

My research has shown me that the full complexity of the orb phenomenon cannot be accounted for under the three ways of reacting with light that I have outlined above: *reflection, absorption,* and *scattering*. The people, buildings, or landscapes that are in the picture with the orbs can be accounted for under these three headings, but not the orbs themselves. What makes the difference in the case of the orbs? Here we are on to an important clue.

Fluorescence: The Major Key to the Nature of Orbs

Once again, my physics classes from long ago came to the rescue. I remembered learning that some objects can absorb light energy transmitted from a source and then later release visible light of a lesser energy when the original light source is no longer transmitting. This process, known as *fluorescence*, gives us a major clue as to the nature of the orbs and the realms they inhabit.

In more technical terms, fluorescence happens when a molecule's electrons are stimulated by an electromagnetic stimulus such as a photon. When the electromagnetic stimuli (photons/light) stop, the excitation of the molecule ceases, and the molecule returns to its resting state. The molecule then expels the electrons that can no longer "fit" into the resting state of the molecule as photons, creating a beam of light.

---

appear so because they are not solid enough to block the light coming from the background behind them, and they do not scatter back the light that strikes them to any significant degree, at least not more than what is sufficient to indicate their presence.

A good example of fluorescence in action is an ordinary sodium vapor streetlamp. The electrical stimulation that powers the lamp causes the sodium gas to fluoresce and emit that yellowish light with which we are all familiar.

Let's apply fluorescence to orb photography.

In orb photography, when light photons from the camera flash strike an orb, they are absorbed by it, thus converting the photons into electrons inside the orb. In colloquial terms this drives the original electrons of the orb up to a higher orbit "shelf."

When the stimulus of the flash ceases, the orb sinks back almost to its original state—somewhat like a balloon being partially deflated—and the "surplus" electrons are expelled again as photons but at a longer wavelength (i.e., a wavelength with a higher number of nm). These expelled electrons that are now photons/light will be detected by the digital camera and recorded as an orb if it falls within a wavelength band that is not beyond that of low infrared (approximately 1,000 nm).

As the light from the fluorescing orb hits the CCD of the camera milliseconds after the reflected light from the flash hits the CCD, the shutter may already be in the process of closing. This means that the light from the orb will be "cropped" by the leaves that make up the shutter of the camera and the orb will be given the shape of said leaves. The light that records the other objects in the photograph will be unaffected, since that light was already recorded by the camera when the shutter was fully open. So only the appearance of the orbs in the photograph will be affected, nothing else.

All of this then is not due to a camera fault—some lack of synchronization between the timing of the shutter and the camera

Examples of hexagonal orbs. The orbs themselves are not hexagons; rather, the camera shutter pattern is imprinted onto these orbs

Figure I-1

Figure I-2

Orbs appear in an incredible variety of shapes, sizes, and colors. The photographs in figures I-3 through I-16A, all of which I have taken myself, are examples of brown, red, white, blue, and pink orbs.

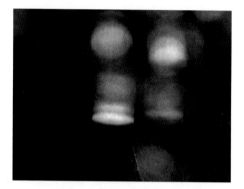

Figure I-3

Figure I-4

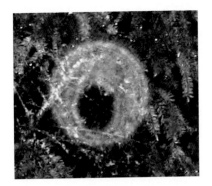

Figure I-5

Figure I-6

Figure I-7

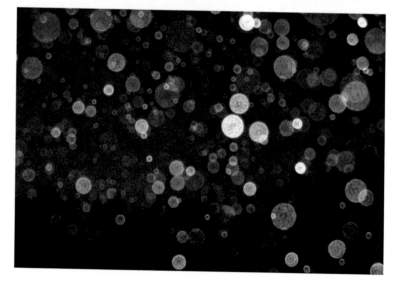

Figure I-8

Figure I-9

Figure I-10

Figure I-11

A little girl and her dog dance beneath colored orbs on a summer's evening.

Figure I-12

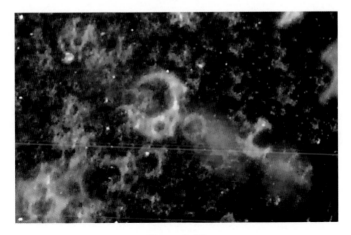

Figure I-13

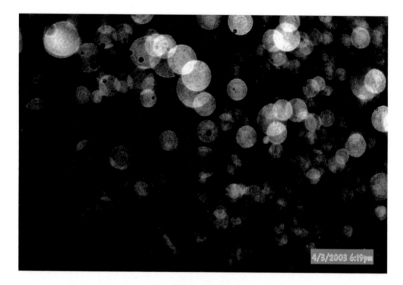

Figure I-14

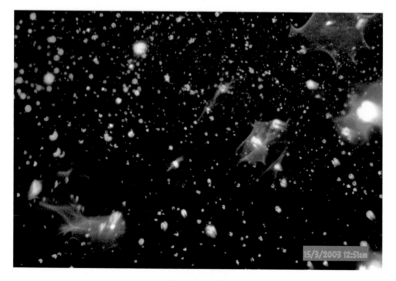

Figure I-15

Figure I-16

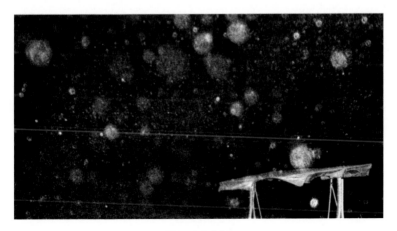

Figure I-16A

Orbs occasionally manifest themselves out of the orb shape into plasma-like clouds. Figures I-17 through I-24 show formations that I call "plasmoids."

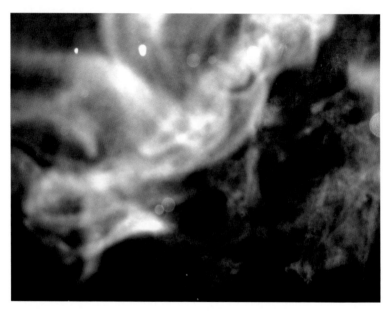

Figure I-17

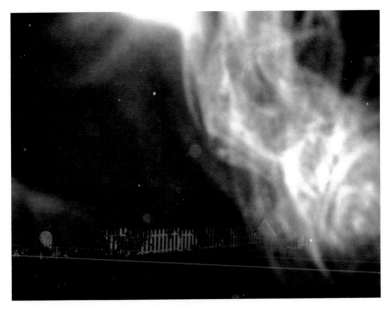

Figure I-18

Figure I-19

Figure I-20

Figure I-21

Figure I-22

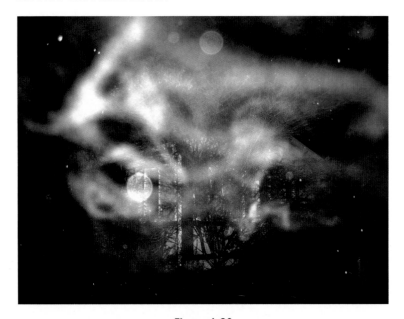

Figure I-23

Figure I-24

These two photographs, taken just ten seconds apart, illustrate orbs forming into plasmoids.

Figure I-25

Figure I-26

Orbs sometimes appear as graceful drapes of fine cloth. I call these "veils."

Figure I-27

Energy spheres, such as the orb in the foreground of this photo, are much larger than the average orb and lack the characteristic dented form. Because the sphere's edge is not clearly defined, these orbs are easily mistaken for water drops.

Figure I-28

Red giants, shown in these photographs, are generally much larger than the average orb and they often have two intense points of red light near their circumference.

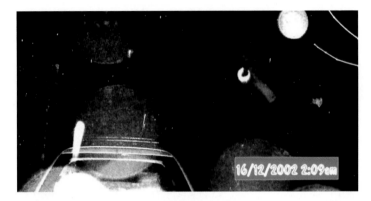

Figure I-29

Figure I-30

A very rare rocket orb.

Figure I-31

Sometimes orbs appear to have segments missing from them. I call these "skeletals." This type of incomplete orb may be due to the fact that the orb has not yet fully manifested into a frequency level that the camera can capture, or is disappearing out of that range.

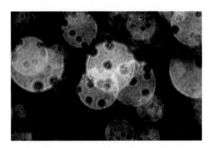

Figure I-32

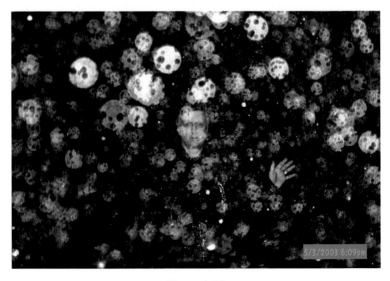

Figure I-33

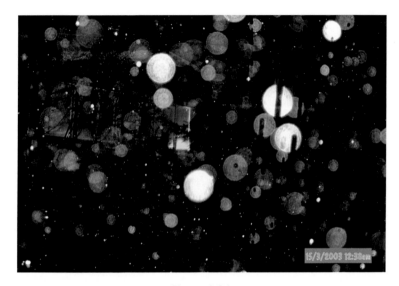

Figure I-34

Figure I-35

Figures I-36 through I-41 show orbs in the process of forming a vortex.

Figure I-36

Figure I-37

Figure I-38

Figure I-39

Figure I-40

A double vortex also formed, with light bands stretching across the diameter.

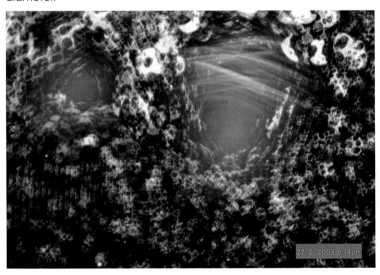

Figure I-41

Orbs that I call "carnival lights" appeared when I began to take pictures straight up into the sky.

Figure I-42

Occasionally an orb will exhibit characteristics different from the other orbs around it. I call these "observational lights." In this photo, the bright orb assumed this unique form while the other orbs assumed the hexagonal form.

Figure I-43

More "observational lights." These orbs assumed this form when the other orbs assumed the spherical form.

Figure I-44

Figure I-44A

Figure I-45

Figure I-46

These "tricolor orbs" exhibit different shades of color around their rims, which indicates the direction in which they are traveling.

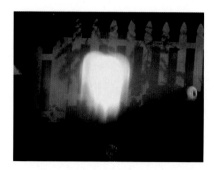

Figure I-47

Figure I-48

Orbs sometimes form images of faces within their spherical shape, as in these photographs.

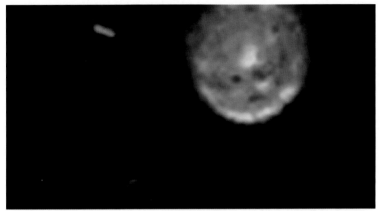

Figure I-49

(Courtesy of JZK, Inc.)

(Courtesy of JZK, Inc.)

Figure I-50

Orbs are frequently found near children and in lighthearted environments, as in this wedding at Ramtha's School of Enlightenment.

(Courtesy of JZK, Inc.)

Figure I-51

This collage shows how orbs appearing at Ramtha's School of Enlightenment assumed a camera-like shape. A photographer's hand was superimposed on the image to aid in identification.

(Courtesy of JZK, Inc.)

Figure I-52

Moisture in the air often facilitates abundant manifestation of orbs. In these conditions, care must be taken not to mistake fog particles for true orb images. This photograph shows orbs in fog. Their interior features offer a clue that they are authentic orbs.

Figure I-53

Examples of orbs with highly detailed interiors. Patterns like these can help identify the orbs from one photographic session to another.

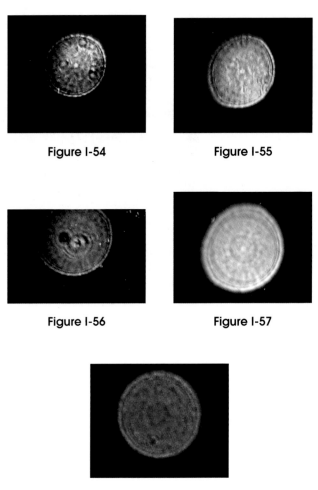

Figure I-54

Figure I-55

Figure I-56

Figure I-57

Figure I-58

flash—but is due simply to a delay in the light from the second light source reaching the camera lens. The reflected light from the flash gets back to the camera while the process of fluorescence is still occurring in the orbs. The light from the fluorescence arrives milliseconds later. As you can see, depending on the speed with which the shutter opens and closes, the fluorescence at times might be sufficiently delayed so that the shutter closes before the fluorescing light is able to reach the camera. In that case the orbs, even if present in multitudes, would not be photographed at all; this, in addition to the problem of "hot mirrors" (which I will explain in chapter 5), could possibly contribute to some otherwise excellent cameras not being suitable for orb photography.

These considerations may also help to explain how orbs of a higher frequency can be captured by a camera unable to detect light that is beyond low-infrared: light expelled during fluorescence is expelled at a longer wavelength. However, the other implications of this fact are much more significant.

After scientists gained a better knowledge of the nature of the atom, the physics of fluorescence was normally applied to substantial and physical realities, such as minerals. However, in minerals fluorescence occurs slowly, presumably because of the density of the material. If fluorescence is what is happening in orb photography, then it must take place almost instantaneously or the orb image could not be captured during the fraction of a second the camera shutter is open. Presumably this can occur because of the much less dense state of the orbs.

So apparently orbs do not *reflect*, *absorb*, or *scatter* light, the three conventional ways in which objects become visible under illumination.

Rather, it seems that the flash's photons stimulate the orbs to absorb the photons, convert them into electrons, and then expel them again as photons of a lower frequency when the stimulus of the flash ceases. Then the orb reverts back to its original dimensions. The lower frequency at which the photons are emitted will be a frequency that is the exact difference between the "excited" state of the orb and the "resting" state. This is an important clue.

So, for example, in taking a nighttime picture in which orbs are present, the majority of the scene—buildings, vegetation, people, pets, and so on—are registered by the camera by the flash's light being reflected back from the objects into the camera lens. By contrast, I am suggesting that the orbs are not registered by the camera through reflection but through fluorescence.

This means that the camera, and in rarer cases the naked eye, is recording low-level photonic emissions just beyond the range of visible light. If orbs manage to collect a significant surplus of electrons by the various mechanisms described in this book, then the discharge of those electrons may sometimes be sufficient to generate a visible light component that may make them visible without apparatus. This may also explain why more orbs are seen after a certain amount of flash photography has taken place than at the beginning of the photographic session.

Further Insights from Fluorescence

If this suggestion is true then it is a fortunate discovery. If the orbs fluoresce, then the quality of light that comes from them may convey information about the level of reality that they inhabit, and we can no longer regard them as ghosts or spirits of the dead.

If orbs fluoresce, it means that in some sense the orbs are physical, even if obviously well beyond the levels of the physical to which we are accustomed. This does not mean that they are not "spiritual" entities; it simply means that our understanding of "spiritual" would stand in sore need of redefinition.

The question posed earlier still remains: What is the significance of the fact that the camera is viewing color that may be from a frequency that is beyond the range of the visible light spectrum? The only apparent answer at this stage of the investigation, now that we have looked at the phenomenon of fluorescence as the most likely mechanism by which orbs are rendered visible, is that the orbs may be "fluorescing" light back to us from within themselves. That light shows in a pale or muted manner the frequencies to which they as objects belong. By analyzing the wavelength of the colors being fluoresced, we can learn more about the object that is fluorescing. If an orb reflects back infrared light, then the orbs as beings must surely belong to the infrared realm or slightly above. If this is so it would indicate the existence of levels of the physical universe other than those that we currently acknowledge or that we acknowledge only as frequency bands.

This was an extremely exciting realization for me since it seemed to corroborate with physical evidence Ramtha's teachings on the nature of reality.[2] Ramtha has explained that creation occurred when

2. Ramtha, the Enlightened One (Spirit), channeled by JZ Knight, *A Beginner's Guide to Creating Reality: An Introduction to Ramtha and His Teachings* (Yelm, Wash.: JZK Publishing, revised and expanded edition, 2000), 111–25.

the primeval Void "contemplated itself."[3] This produced what Ramtha termed "Point Zero."[4] When Point Zero in turn contemplated itself, it produced another reality: time, distance, and space.[5] This is how the seventh plane of reality emerged, where time is very rapid. Now "Point Zero" needs to get this (mirror consciousness) message to do the same. So time between Point Zero and its mirror consciousness on the seventh plane is collapsed and the next contemplation is of a plane of reality slower in frequency and time, the sixth plane of reality.[6] We now "have a ladder being built."[7] This process continues until the fifth, fourth, third, second, and first levels of reality have been created, each level decreasing in frequency. The last level constitutes the lowest and slowest of the planes, which is the physical one we inhabit.

Comparing Color, Wavelength, Electron Voltage, and Frequency

The following table, which shows how color is related to wavelength, voltage, and frequency, will help you better understand the nature and significance of the different colored orbs we capture on camera.

The energy of light photons is measured in electrons volts; an energy of less than 1.65 electron volts will radiate photons of infrared color. An energy of more than 3.26 electron volts will radiate in the

3. Ibid., 113.
4. Ibid., 116.
5. Ibid., 116.
6. Ibid., 117.
7. Ibid., 118.

Color	Wavelength	Elect. Voltage	Frequency
UV Light	200 to 300 nm	3.33 to 5.00	6.20 to 4.15
Visible Light	420 to 700 nm	2.95 to 1.77	6.38 to 4.28
Violet			
Blue			
Green			
Yellow			
Red			
Infrared Light	1,000 nm	1.24	3.00

ultraviolet part of the spectrum, a wavelength way below (or much too short) for the human brain to see normally. It is also beyond the reach of conventional digital cameras.

We are normally dependent on a device such as a digital camera to detect anything higher in wavelength than about 780 nm (in equivalent terms, lower than 1.65 in electron voltage, or lower than about 3.00 terahertz in frequency). The existence of the light frequencies that the orbs fluoresce seems to indicate a realm of existence that corresponds to those electron voltages, frequencies, and wavelengths that Ramtha described. In short, the colors mediated to the camera through the low infrared band suggest the existence of realms that may be distinguished from one another by shorter and shorter wavelengths as frequencies rise. So the range of colors that the orbs exhibit in digital photographs may very well be evidence of the existence of energy frequency realms to which the various categories of orbs belong. These realms are seen as frequencies by us, whereas in this hypothesis they would be not just frequencies but actual realms

of existence, just as our own realm of existence here might be perceived "just" as a frequency by those "above" us.

What Are the Implications of This Discovery?

If the range of colors that the orbs display are a clue to the planes of
existence they inhabit, it is clear that the realms of existence we used
to call "the beyond" are no less wonderful than we thought (and are
in fact far more wonderful than we thought), but they are now less
mysterious. It is equally clear that if these are the realms the entities
we choose to call "spirits" inhabit, they are very different indeed from
what was envisaged by most agencies that taught and discussed these
matters in the past, including the religious traditions.

Now we may begin to see that mystery should perhaps not be understood as absurdity, something that totally baffles the mind (which is the
way the word is normally understood), but rather as something that is too
large for the mind to comprehend more than partially, at least for now.

The idea that there is no stability as we know it in the world, but
that reality is just an endless series of becomings, was well known in
Greek philosophy, principally in the work of Heraclitus, the most
significant Greek philosopher after Plato and Aristotle, in the late
sixth century B.C. It was largely ignored in those later developments
of Greek thought that influenced the thinking of Western Europe.

In a similar vein, for scientist David Bohm[8] (1917–94), the world
of matter and the experience of consciousness were simply two

---

8. David Bohm, *Quantum Theory* (New York: Prentice-Hall, 1951); *Wholeness and the Implicate Order* (London, Boston: Routledge and Kegan Paul, 1980); *Thought as a System* (London, New York: Routledge, 1994).

aspects of a more fundamental process he called "the implicate order." According to Bohm, both the theories of relativity and quantum theory, if carried to extremes, violate every present-day notion on which our idea of reality is based.

But the wider perspective suggested by these frames of thought, which might provide a framework on what the orbs and their native realms may be, does not come easy to us, not least because of the inadequacy of the traditional labels we have customarily used, such as "the dead" or "spirits."

We all carry unconscious prejudices and limitations from both our secular and religious cultures, and these can bedevil the chances of any balanced and objective understanding of what the orb phenomenon means for us. Those who come from a religious background will instinctively tend to see the orb entities merely as beings of pure spirit, or as spirits of the dead in some form, or as ghosts or demons, and approach the question with all of the baggage that superstition brings with it from those traditions. This in turn is overlaid with traces of the limited and bizarre way in which the secular Western world today views any supposed dimension beyond this material one—usually as Halloween hauntings, vampires, ghouls, creatures that ooze slime, or fearsome extraterrestrials. The lenses of prejudice, superstition, fear, and—worst of all—fanaticism through which phenomena such as this are normally viewed have given rise to many curious and badly defined descriptions, such as "the supernatural," "the paranormal," or "the occult," all terms that reveal far more about our fears and superstitions than they do about the true nature of these other realities. There is less of the occult in the orb phenomena than there is in you and me.

If those persons who have lost their bodies through physical death inhabit one or more of these realms that orb fluorescence indicates, then the afterlife is a very different condition indeed from what has been traditionally imagined and taught.

If the range of color harmonics the fluorescing orbs display is a clue to the levels of energy frequency to which they belong, it seems very likely that most of the orbs we photograph may never have been incarnated in a physical body on this earth at all, or indeed anywhere else in this material dimension. In my experience, most orbs of the "dead" tend to be in infrared or the light realm, not in the ultraviolet, gamma, or x-ray frequencies. So orbs of higher colors (especially gold, rose, and silver) are most likely of beings that have never incarnated materially in this physical plane. So it seems the study of orbs or their plasmoid forms may have little to do with ghosts but everything to do with learning more about the nature of the complex realities that abut onto our own fields of existence. These other realities have profound implications for how we understand ourselves and our place in the cosmos.

Enormous Variety of
Orb Manifestation

Before we go into the great variety of orbs that have appeared in my photographs, I'd like to summarize the pieces of the puzzle that led me to my preliminary conclusions about the nature of the orbs and the other related phenomena.

If the orbs through fluorescence produce from within themselves a light that at least in part must belong to the near-infrared spectrum, then that may indicate two things.

First, the orbs are not composed of some ethereal substance like the ectoplasm that was an essential feature of the spiritualistic séances popular in the nineteenth and early twentieth centuries.[1] If a process of fluorescence aided by the attraction of free electrons through ionization is what enables the orbs to be photographed,

---

1. *Ekto* and *plasma* are the Greek words for "exteriorized substance."

then the orbs must be *electromagnetic* in nature, and *most likely are energy fields of some kind*.

Second, if they produce a radiation that is at least partly infrared, then they must belong to a realm that is at least at the frequency/wavelength of infrared or beyond. This indicates that the orbs are native to the dimensions that lie in frequency levels above our material realm. Normally, then, they will be manifested in this dimension only when a process occurs that causes them to give off a level of radiation a camera could perceive, especially one that is sensitive to infrared.

If an orb can only be photographed when its light radiation is lowered to the bottom end of the infrared spectrum, it would explain why a much greater lowering of its frequency would be necessary for it to be photographed with normal film and why far fewer orbs can be captured on film rather than on the digital CCD. If there are orbs in the frequency levels above infrared, then they can only be captured by a normal digital camera if their frequency is lowered to low infrared. This lowering would probably dim the intensity of their colors, but they would probably still retain the colors that betrayed their frequencies of origin.

With these conclusions in mind, let's turn our attention to the different types of orbs that I have observed. I will attempt to classify the orbs and show examples of each so that you will be better able to recognize and identify orbs yourself.

Classifying Orbs

St. Thomas More, Lord Chancellor of England under Henry VIII, once said of a problem on which he was working: "It's like trying to

44

milk a he-goat into a sieve." The same can be said of attempts to survey or categorize the types and variety of forms that make up the orb phenomenon. With each week that passes, new varieties and new phenomena appear. The orbs associated with other levels of reality beyond this one seem to engage in different functions and also seem to show different energetic levels, which probably accounts for the colors they exhibit. Beside color and size variations many other forms are met as well; the ones I have encountered are outlined below.

Brown, red, white, blue, and pink orbs

Figures I-3 through I-16A show examples of orbs in this color range. Orbs that may be associated with the infrared realm (the realm immediately above the physical) have a reddish brown tinge. Orbs of presumably other levels manifest in varying shades of white, ultraviolet blue, gold, and rose. Orbs that appear as translucent or almost entirely clear may be on the verge of passing out of the realm of detection altogether. Orbs that are of the higher frequencies, or that may even be approaching the quantum field itself (sixth plane), will be much smaller in terms of apparent size but obviously are of a much higher frequency and consequently of greater power.

Plasmoid fields of different colors

On occasion the orbs seem able to manifest themselves out of the orb shape into plasma-like clouds (see figures I-17 through I-26). Plasma has been called in popular jargon "the fourth state of matter" following solids, liquids, and gases. This may be what this form of orb manifestation is, so I call them plasma fields or "plasmoids." Plasma consists of a set of free-moving electrons and ions, which are atoms that have lost electrons. Energy is needed so that plasma can be formed and maintained, and that energy can come from heat, electricity, or intense laser light. In the orb manifestations frequently these clouds can assume the shapes of familiar forms, sometimes undeniably of the human face. It seems to be difficult to accomplish this or to hold the pattern for more than a brief period; the energy requirements just mentioned would explain this. To my request to form a certain shape, they have on occasion responded positively. These plasmoid clouds are normally of the same color and frequency as the orbs from which they emanate.

Figures I-25 and I-26 illustrate plasmoids forming out of orbs within a space of ten seconds, which was the time that separated the taking of these two pictures. Capturing this transmutation is a rarely photographed phenomenon.

Veils

Occasionally objects that resemble graceful drapes of fine cloth appear in attractive formations. See figure I-27. I do not know what causes this, but it is not a camera fault or a fault in technique on the part of the photographer.

Energy spheres

Take a look at figure I-28. These energy spheres are much larger than the average orb and do not have the characteristic dented circular form. The edge of the sphere is fluffy rather than clearly defined. Care needs to be taken not to confuse them with distortions caused by drops of water on the camera lens.

Red giants

Red Giants sometimes have two intense points of red light near their circumference. On closer examination of a large number of pictures, on certain nights this type of orb was the dominant kind to show up. To estimate the size of an orb is always difficult since a small orb close to the camera will seem much larger than a very large orb at some distance away. In figure I-29, a car was parked against a line of trees and the orbs here are approximately of the same width as the car.

Red Giants are generally much larger than the more usual form of orbs; I have been able to calculate an average diameter for them of about five or six feet and on one occasion a diameter of more than ten feet, as in figure I-30.

One of the central insights of quantum physics is that the effect of the observer on the quantum field will cause reality to reorganize itself according to the observation and that observed reality must then descend through the frequency levels below the quantum field before it reaches density in material reality.

If the orbs lack the characteristic circles inside the outer circumference, I wondered whether they are likely to be observational thought forms that have descended from the quantum field and are about to pop into physical manifestation in the physical plane. This would square well with the basic insights of quantum physics, and as such realities presumably must at some stage be detectable before they arrive at the level of the physical, it is worth at least pondering what this form of orb might be and whether it fits into that category, since the near-infrared vibration of these objects would be characteristic of an object in the closest stage to physical manifestation. As I've mentioned, the dark-red orbs I have photographed in this category are extremely large, which may indicate they were in a stage close to visible physical manifestation.

Rocket orb

Figure I-31 is of what I call a "rocket orb." This type of orb is very rare, and I have only encountered it twice in the years I have been taking these pictures. On the first occasion, it was the last picture that particular digital camera ever took, but I am not sure if that could be attributed to this intense orb form or not.

Skeletals

Figures I-32 through I-35 are examples of skeletals—orbs that appear to have holes or segments missing. Various explanations have been advanced to explain this; one psychic pronounced that there had been a war between the orbs and that these holes and "missing" parts were the results of damage suffered in those conflicts! I think that theory may be abandoned without too much risk. Even if such a conflict had taken place, "damage" to these energy bodies would much more likely take the form of a slowing of frequency or a change in color or intensity than in any physical-style gaps or holes in its structure. This type of apparently "damaged" or incomplete orb may be due to the fact that the orb has not yet fully manifested into a level of frequency that the camera can capture, or is disappearing out of that range, so that the gaps we see in those orbs are not actually in them but in our perception of them.

Vortices and torsion fields with the conditions that precede them

On many occasions I noticed strange formations beginning to take shape, where the orbs' skeletal form appeared to rotate around a central core into which the orbs were gradually drawn. They totally lost their form in the process, appearing almost like pieces of white rag (see figures I-36 and I-37).

This process gradually accelerated until a clearly defined vortex was formed (see figures I-38 through I-41). From where I stood to the core of the vortex measured about eleven feet. I am not aware that such orb pictures have been captured elsewhere.

In figure I-41, you can see that a double vortex also formed, with light bands arching across the diameter of the cone shape. Two symbols are of significance here. First, the orbs seem to assume the shape and rotation of a torsion vortex. Second, someone suggested to me that the skeletal symbolism might be a reference to death and also that the spinning tunnel-like vortex may be the spiral reported by those who have undergone near-death experiences.

Carnival lights

When I began to take pictures straight up into the sky, I frequently obtained pictures such as figure I-42, which I named "carnival lights." When I came upon pictures taken by the Hubble Space Telescope, I noticed how dramatically similar these orb pictures were to the distant space bodies captured by the telescope.

Observational orbs

On occasion an orb started to exhibit quite different behavior patterns. In these examples an entirely different shape appeared when the orbs assumed the hexagonal form. In figure I-43, the orb shows the form it assumed that is visible in the first picture when the orbs assumed the hexagonal form. Figures I-44A, I-45, and I-46 show the form it assumed when the other orbs assumed the spherical form.

Tricolor orbs

Take a look at figures I-47 and I-48. Many of the orbs exhibit different shades of color around their rims, which indicates the direction in which they are traveling. Generally speaking, a blue shade seems to appear in the direction the orb is traveling, and a brownish or red shade appears in the direction from which it has come.

Images within the orbs

On many occasions spherical orb forms have managed to form images of faces (see figures I-49 and I-50).

Figure I-51 was taken at Ramtha's School of Enlightenment during a wedding ceremony. An orb distinctly showing a child's face appears behind the young couple. (It is noteworthy that orbs rarely frequent places where the atmosphere is gloomy and seem particularly attracted to where children play or the environment is lighthearted).

On one occasion at Ramtha's School of Enlightenment when orbs were first being photographed there, a series of pictures showed the orbs assuming camera-like shapes, presumably issuing an invitation to take more photographs of them! In the rendition in figure I-52, the camera that was used is shown on the top left. A photographer's hand has been superimposed on the image of the camera-like orb in order to more clearly identify the orbs' features.

Orbs in fog

Humidity, cold, and dampness facilitate abundant manifestation of orbs. Care must be taken that fog particles, raindrops, and dust are not confused with true orb images. Figure I-53 is an example of orbs in fog.

Most orbs seem to have a line or lines visible a small distance inside their circumference, which might indicate that they were flat in nature rather than spherical, and this helps to separate true orb pictures from false. However, after even a relatively small experience in this field you will find it easier to know what is really an orb and what is due to one or more of the unwanted effects mentioned above.

Orbs usually exhibit concentric circle formations inside their outer circumference as well as peculiar systems of knobs and bumps on their face. See figures I-54 through I-58 for examples of highly detailed orbs. These patterns, which seem to be as individual as human fingerprints, can serve to identify the orbs from one photographic session to another. Be observant of the varied features exhibited by the orbs you photograph and you will get a greater sense of the enormous variety of orb manifestations.

4

Vortices and Torsion Fields:
Orbs That May Not Be Electromagnetic

In the latter half of the twentieth century, scientists believed that all of nature's observable phenomena could be explained by the four known interactions: electromagnetism, gravity, and the strong and weak nuclear forces. The appearance of experimental results that could not be explained in terms of these four known interactions pointed to the existence of torsion effects, which changed our ideas of how the world is organized.

Many scientists now believe that all substances possess their own torsion field. Torsion waves can travel at speeds in excess of the speed of light and there is no loss of speed as the waves spread. This phenomenon could make long-distance communication possible across the galaxy, without signal deterioration. In torsion fields, like charges are attracted to each other, which is the opposite of what happens in electromagnetism, where like charges repel and opposite charges attract. This new paradigm opens the possibility of obtaining critically new results in all scientific and technological areas, so that the characteristic technologies of the twenty-first century may well be torsion technologies.

The Impact of the Torsion Field on Gravity and Light

Gravitational fields and torsion fields have some properties in common. Neither can be shielded by natural materials. A gravitational field is identical to the *longitudinal* spin polarization of the physical vacuum, while a torsion field is identical to the *transverse* spin polarization of the physical vacuum.[1] It is possible to block torsion fields by some artificial materials; for example, two crossed sheets of ordinary polyethylene film. This plastic is made in such a way that the polymers form an aligned unidirectional structure, which results in a molecular spin ordering. The outcome is the generation of a collective torsion field. Two crossed polyethylene films are transparent to most of the radio frequency wave spectrum, but they can block torsion radiation.

Torsion radiation of a physical material will result only in the alteration of its spin state. However, an alteration of the spin state of the physical vacuum can result in changes to the polarization angle of a light beam. I believe this is of central relevance in explaining

---

1. Y. V. Nachalov and E. A. Parkhomov, "Experimental Detection of the Torsion Field," http://www.amasci.com/freenrg/tors/doc15.html.

some effects in the distortion of physical realities I noted during my study and are recorded in several photographs in this book. (It is noteworthy that changes to a substance's spin state also cause changes in its ability to be magnetized.)

The relevance of all this to the study of orbs is that a torsion field can change the rate of any physical process. This is most notable in the effect on quartz crystals: Their oscillation frequency is significantly changed when they are subjected to a torsion field. Experiments with the quartz crystals seemed to assume a relationship between the torsion field and the distortion of time. If the torsion field and the gravitational field operate in different directions to each other, and if we accept that time is a vector of the magnetic field, then this poses tantalizing questions about the effect of a torsion field on time.

If a torsion field is superimposed on a gravitational field in a certain area, it may result in the reduction of gravity in that area. That means the influence of torsion radiation on a physical object may result in a reduction of that object's weight. That property of torsion fields was discovered in the 1950s by N. A. Kozyrev and later confirmed by experiments conducted by others.[2] A prime example is when a person levitates. This occurs because the torsion field, which works in the opposite direction to the gravitational field, is now

2. Nikolai Alexandrovich Kozyrev, *Izbrannyye trudy* (Selected works) (Leningrad State University, 1991), (in Russian); A. I. Veinik, *Termodinamika realnykh protsessov* (Thermodynamics of real processes) (Minsk: Nauka i Tekhnika, 1991), (in Russian); and M. M. Lavrentiev et al., *O registratsii reaktsii veshestva na vneshnii neobratimyi protsess* (On registration of substance reaction to an external irreversible process) (Doklady AN SSSR, vol. 317, no. 3, 1991), (in Russian); cited in Nachalov and Parkhomov, http://www.amasci .com/freenrg/tors/doc15.html.

canceling out the effect for the gravitational attraction on the body, so the person becomes weightless.

If any substance—be it the physical vacuum, the human body, or even a physical location—is subjected to the influence of an external torsion field, this will cause a transverse spin polarization of that substance. The torsion field can be "recorded" in the physical object subject to the external torsion radiation. This effect can last for many months if the torsion effect that has been recorded is shielded by a device like the crossed plastic sheets mentioned earlier. If the charged object is subjected to any physical shocks, the torsion charge will disappear because the torsion fields are closely coupled to inertial forces.

A Torsion Vortex Produced by Orbs?

As you can see in figures I-36 through I-41, I have photographed what I believe to be conditions that led to the forming of a full-fledged torsion vortex. I took about twenty photographs of the vortices that appeared that first night, and on several subsequent occasions I have photographed the earlier stages of the processes manifesting again. As I do not understand precisely how the phenomenon was generated by what I did, the best course of action is to describe in detail what circumstances I noted leading up to this manifestation. As our knowledge of this phenomenon develops we will be better able to judge which circumstance was of greater or lesser importance—and which may have been of no importance at all.

A few days before the first manifestation of the vortex, I was attempting to take a photograph of an area bound by trees, about fifty yards in front of me in my driveway. It was in the afternoon, broad daylight. When I pressed the button, instead of the photograph being taken straightaway, as would normally happen, the infrared rangefinder on the camera started to adjust the length of the lens. It was as if there was some object close up in front of me that I could not see but that the infrared beam of the camera rangefinder detected and on which it focused the lens. However, no image of anything closer than the trees came out in the photograph.

As I went on down the drive and came near to the trees I took some more pictures. This time I could see with my naked eyes a large orb-like object against, or in, the trees. It seemed to be about twenty or thirty feet in height and the same in width.

I have been a keen amateur photographer for more than forty years and long ago learned all the little blunders that could ruin our pictures: avoid moving the camera while taking pictures, make sure the object is in focus, and so on. However, my camera was an auto-focus model, and I had never had a blurred picture with it over the three years I had used it. Yet directly after I detected this large object I had four or five photographs in a row that were out of focus or distorted in some way. One of the picket fence along my driveway showed the vertical white fence boards duplicated about a foot or two above the actual fence. At the time I dismissed this picture as due to some very rudimentary mistake I had made, such as moving the camera in a downward direction just as I was taking the shot, and thought no more of it for a few days. Fortunately I did not delete the "faulty" pictures.

Moving to another part of my yard I was able to see areas against the trees that seemed to be hazy or blurred. I photographed them and registered the "blurs" but thought at first that it might be due to raindrops on the lens. And though a few drops of rain were falling, the lens was perfectly dry when I checked it. All of this took place in daylight.

The next night when I began the photographic session, some quite strange phenomena started to appear. If I had not had some good instruction on what the orbs were I might have felt I was attracting the attention of some shady characters from the nether world and packed up the whole endeavor to retreat to the safety of my house. As I mentioned earlier, I had photographed numerous pictures of orbs that seemed to have holes in them or segments "missing." Those effects were not due to any deficiencies in the orbs themselves—and certainly not due to war damage among the orbs! No, what appeared now was far more bizarre than that. Orbs appeared that displayed striking deformities; they were fragmented, with large "holes," stretchings, and distortions of all kinds. Over a period of about half an hour what remained of the orb shapes started to spin around a center formed by a gray energy sphere, which did not have defined edges such as the orbs have. The orbs by this time appeared like ragged pieces of white cloth, as you can see in figure I-37. Within a short while a clearly defined spinning vortex with an energy sphere at its center developed. Given the phenomenon's characteristics it is entirely possible that what was photographed dozens of times may have been a torsion field developing, which conceivably might exert on adjacent objects the properties and effects of the torsion fields I have just described.

During my photography session the following night, the same phenomena appeared again, this time after a much shorter period of time. This may have been due to the "imprinting effect" of the torsion field, which I have referred to above, which would make the generation of the field subsequently an easier process. Quite soon a fully developed vortex appeared. I measured with my hands the size of the energy sphere at its center, and it was about two and a half to three feet in diameter. The sides of the spinning vortex, composed now of orbs that had almost entirely disintegrated from their original shape, extended back from the energy sphere toward the camera about twelve to fifteen feet.

Over the next few days I conducted my photography session in the same area, but in daylight. I noted some distortions of the physical reality before the camera that could not be explained by camera shake or movement of the person or object in the camera's field of view. These orb forms were accompanied by other phenomena that resemble spiked or pyramid-shaped "veils," which appeared on many photographs, taken both during the night and also in broad daylight.

Further Investigation

The orbs we have studied are themselves electromagnetic in nature (proven by their fluorescence when photonic stimulation was applied to them), and it is to be expected that they can affect and control the electromagnetic charges that record the images in digital photography. As a result of various experiments I have conducted, I now have sufficient data to show that they can manipulate the electromagnetic charges being recorded.

Future experiments could include using a number of machines to ionize the air (in dry conditions) and see if an effect similar to that produced in damp conditions can be achieved. An ionizing meter is in fact one of the most useful corroborating devices for the presence of orbs, as a change in ionization seems to accompany their appearance. An ordinary gauss meter, which measures gravitational fields, is also a useful detection tool.

Extensive use of powerful strobe lighting at all times during the photographic session also enhances the amount of orbs in pictures, presumably because of the increased capacity for fluorescence that the pulsed photons of the strobe generate in the orbs.

The discovery that orbs may be forming a torsion vortex opens up very interesting possibilities for our understanding of the nature of reality. The effect that a torsion field may have in warping the time-space fabric is of particular interest and an area that deserves further research. In the next chapter, we will turn our attention to fundamentals of orb photography.

5

Tips for
Photographing Orbs

Photographing orbs is not an arcane or esoteric science, or the preserve of mystics, gurus, or those who fancy themselves favored by God. It is as practical and down-to-earth as can be. Anyone who has sufficient patience and dedication can take orb and plasmoid pictures for themselves and thus have firsthand experience of the evidence. I offer tips from my own extensive study to help you get the most out of your experience.

Digital or Film Cameras?

The basic structure of digital and film cameras is the same. In both types, light comes through the lens, where it is focused onto a receiving medium, which then records it. Both types of camera have shutters that can operate at various speeds to open and close the lens. In modern cameras designed for popular use, the camera automatically selects the shutter speed. The speed is governed by the sensitivity of the recording medium and the amount of light available at the time, which is measured by the camera's light meter. If an object to be photographed is moving rapidly, then a higher speed is desirable to "freeze" the movement and avoid a blurred image.

The digital cameras used for taking the orb photographs in this book were fully automatic, so I had no control over shutter speed or exposure. This is why you see blurred contrails behind orbs in many photographs: The shutter speed was too slow to "freeze" the image of the orb where it was.

If we know the duration of a camera flash—say, typically about 1/1000th of a second—you can easily calculate some rough approximation of the orbs' speed if their distance from the camera is known. For example, if you know an orb is five feet from the camera, and it passes through a distance of say twenty feet during the duration of the flash, then you can readily grasp the enormous speeds at which they can move.

Some people have suggested that such "zooming" orbs may be discharges of energy. A digital movie will yield even better results. An orb movie can be successfully made with a digital movie camera that allows the hot mirrors (which filter out infrared light) to be deactivated, but this has the disadvantage of giving the pictures a greenish tinge. It is probably preferable to do this by using a digital movie camera in conjunction with a powerful strobe, which would take the place of the still camera's flash and cause the orbs to fluoresce.

The receiving and recording medium in cameras is where the major difference between film and digital cameras begins. Film cameras record the image onto a film coated with emulsion containing light-sensitive silver halide crystals. When a beam of light strikes the emulsion, the crystals undergo a chemical change, which records that portion of the image. The image is still hidden, but it is revealed later when the film is immersed in a chemical bath during processing. In black-and-white photography, the processing converts those silver halide clusters that have been hit by the light beams into black metallic silver clusters, which produce a visible image. A more complex but analogous process is used in color film processing.

In digital cameras, the image formed by the lens does not strike a film but a chip array called a charge-coupled device, or CCD. A CCD is a collection of an enormous number of diodes and silicon dots, called photosites. When a light beam strikes the silicon dots (pixels) on the CCD, they react to the light, just like the silver halide crystals do in black-and-white film photography. However, when the light strikes the silicon dots of the CCD, it does not cause a chemical change as it would on film. Instead the light photons are converted into electrons, and the electrical charge is stored on the silicon dots. The more of these dots, or pixels, on the CCD array, obviously the finer the picture quality will be. The intensity of the electrical charges registered and stored on the photosites are proportionate to the intensity of the beam of light photons. Typically a system can support 65,535 colors, and there will be a separate identifiable electrical charge corresponding to each shade of color recorded.

In the past other cameras used a technology known as CMOS (complementary metal oxide semiconductor), not CCD. This produced a lesser-quality picture than the CCD did, plus these older cameras weren't suitable for recording orb images. Because of the inherent deficiencies in CMOS, CCDs became the norm in digital still and movie cameras, astronomical telescopes, and many other functions that require imagery of the highest quality. But that situation is changing. The image quality of CMOS is now matching most CCDs, and since the cost of fabricating a CMOS wafer is only about one-third of the cost of making a similar CCD wafer, CMOS can only gain in popularity.

Digital camera technology is evolving at an enormous speed and there is no foreseeable end in sight. Obviously while higher pixellation has the very welcome result of giving pictures more definition, it also requires a great deal more disc space to store the images.

When an image is captured on a digital camera's CCD array, it then has to be transferred somewhere else for storage before the camera can take another picture. This storage is usually done on small, removable, high-tech discs that come in the same capacities already well familiar to us from computers.

The time the camera takes to move the image from the CCD into storage so that the camera is ready to take another picture is called the recycling time. That time depends on the speed of the camera processor and other factors, and waiting for the recycling process to finish can be one of the most frustrating experiences in orb photography. When you see a remarkable result in a picture just taken, the wait until another picture can be taken can seem like an eternity. In this area, just as in every other, you only get what you pay for, which is one of the reasons you should buy the best camera you can afford—provided, of course, you first test it for sensitivity to light outside the range our eyes can see. (This procedure will be described shortly.)

One enormous advantage that a digital camera has over its film counterparts in orb photography is that the digital camera CCD is just as sensitive to that part of the light spectrum known as "near-infrared" as it is to visible light. Near-infrared, as explained earlier, are the frequencies just beneath visible red light, which begin about wavelength 700 nm. It seems that these are near the lower end of the frequencies in which orbs become visible. Normal camera film is not sensitive to these frequencies. This is one of the reasons why people who use digital cameras tend to get more orb images than those who use film cameras—because the light from the orbs, which is in the low infrared frequency, can only be captured on a digital CCD.

The difficulty in obtaining orb pictures with sophisticated and expensive digital cameras has been pointed out by others, but those who did so were intent on drawing a different conclusion from mine. It is true that more expensive cameras have antireflective coatings on the lens to reduce "ghost" reflections, and baffles to trap stray reflections within the lens, but it is not correct to say, "This is the main reason why these phenomena (i.e., orb photographs) are seen more in the low-end cameras, and why there has been such a huge proliferation in the number of orbic and anomalous photographs being circulated."[1] The much more likely explanation is this: more expensive cameras are

1. Schwartz and Creath, in *Journal of Scientific Exploration* 19, no. 3 (2005), 355.

very likely to have an elaborate system of "hot mirrors" installed, to improve the quality of normal pictures by filtering out the near-infrared light (hence "hot").

Unfortunately these hot mirror filters also make the camera less sensitive, or not sensitive at all, to images that fall in the near-infrared spectrum, so that an expensive camera that has not been specially modified is unlikely to be able to capture well those orb phenomena that are near-infrared in character. It has nothing to do with an expensive camera having more sophisticated devices to reduce such things as lens flare and stray reflections. This gadgetry would only exclude false orb images.

Hot Mirrors: The Bane of Orb Photography

The near-infrared sensitivity of the CCD, which is so favorable to orb photography, poses problems for normal digital photography, and if left uncorrected it may produce photographs in which the colors appear grainy, distorted, or washed-out. Camera manufacturers normally install a filter into their cameras to reduce the amount of infrared light being admitted to the CCD. This filter, usually a piece of light blue, optical-quality glass, is called by various names: "hot mirror," infrared blocking filter, or, simply, IR (infrared) filter.

Depending on the strength of these filters, very little or no infrared light may be able to get through. As the megapixel capacity of cameras has increased, most manufacturers appear to have installed hot mirrors that are stronger and stronger. If you want to purchase a camera that is capable of taking good orb pictures, it's essential not to forget that near-infrared light and the frequencies very close to it outside of the visible spectrum are what make orbs visible to the camera. So it is obviously very important to buy a camera whose hot mirror does not block out the light from outside the visible spectrum coming in through the lens.

Even if hot mirrors are installed, fortunately I have a test that makes it easy to know whether a camera is still capable of recording near-infrared light. This method will not do much to increase your popularity with local camera salesmen, but it will prevent you buying an expensive camera that is useless for taking orb pictures.

Most ordinary TV remote controls operate by sending out a near-infrared or infrared beam. Bring your remote control to the camera shop. Turn on the camera you are thinking of buying, but be warned that you will often have to ask the salesman to install the camera's battery, which is not always readily available. Hold the camera in one hand and use the other to point the remote straight into the lens of the camera and press some buttons, just as you would do when using it to operate your television set. Look at the screen on the back of the camera. You should see a "bloom" of light, constant or flashing, coming from the remote when you press its buttons. If you see that bloom of light, then your camera's hot mirror will still admit an acceptable amount of near-infrared light to make orb photography possible and rewarding. The bigger the flare of light that you see on your camera's screen, the more sensitive your camera will be to near-infrared light, and hence the better it will be at detecting and recording orb images.

Some people have tried to actually remove the hot mirror. This is neither advisable nor necessary, and it is most certainly not a job for the fainthearted. In the first place, it is not necessary to have just pure infrared light when taking orb photographs, which would have its own downside. A mixture of infrared and visible light will do fine. There are a few cameras available in which the hot mirror can be disengaged manually, but that setting can only be used for night photography. Trying to remove the hot mirror is a technically very difficult process, and it is most definitely not recommended.

If you did want to experiment with a camera that can manually disengage the infrared filters, Sony manufactures suitable cameras. In these cameras, when the "NightShot" mode is selected, the hot mirror is mechanically moved aside, and the change in focus required is compensated for automatically. Caution: the lens opens up wide in this mode and only shutter speeds of 1/30th and 1/60th of a second are available. If you select this mode in daylight you will get very overexposed pictures—useless for our purposes. Sony made this modification because they had attracted a lot of unwelcome publicity when it was alleged (falsely) that the NightShot mode could see through people's clothing in daylight. The truth, apparently, is that cameras using NightShot could pick up the outline of a person's body in wet swimwear. The result has been the loss of the daylight infrared capability of these excellent cameras.

In summary, pure infrared photography and orb photography are not the same thing, so it is not necessary to have a camera that is sensitive only to infrared light in order to take excellent orb pictures. I have tested most of the main camera makes in the 3 to 10 megapixel (MP) range, and most of them work quite well for orb photography.

However, for now the only sure guide is to use the infrared TV remote control test on any new camera you are thinking of purchasing, because the day is not near when the camera makers will start including in their specifications how suitable a camera is for taking orb photographs.

The different forms of orb entities normally all seem to radiate at least in the high regions of hertzian and the near-infrared spectra. As I've explained, it appears that the orbs themselves are electromagnetic in nature. The fact that the CCDs of the digital cameras are near-infrared sensitive, combined with the fact that their recording technology is electromagnetically based, makes digital cameras far superior to film cameras for this work. There are of course also other important factors that favor digital over film: With digital cameras you can see what the results are straightaway. Film images have to wait for processing unless you are using Polaroid. Plus, successful orb photography normally involves the taking of a very large number of pictures, which costs next to nothing with digital after the basic equipment has been bought, whereas it would take very deep pockets to fund the project if film were being used.

As I said earlier, quite amazing results can be obtained in technical effects by tampering with digital images if you have the necessary skill. What is not quite so well known is that it is not difficult to trace and expose attempts at fakery. When a digital picture is taken, the camera creates an EXIF file, which is embedded along with the code for the picture itself. The EXIF records the date and time, and shutter speed and lens aperture settings, as well as the camera make and model. This file will also record and store any subsequent changes made to the image—so altering digital images leaves behind a log of all the changes, which an expert can easily access.

I have included this information here at the risk of being somewhat over-technical because people who are skeptical about the genuineness of the orb phenomenon will only accept evidence that is recorded on film. While it is true that digital images are more easily manipulated than film images, it is also true that only digital photographs record a trail of everything that was done to the image since it was first taken.

6

Distinguishing False Orb Pictures from Real

I f orb pictures were being taken by only a few individuals throughout the world, then this part of the book would be of central importance. However, as I noted earlier, you do not need to be psychic or gifted or favored in some special way by God to take quite exceptional orb pictures. All you need is a lot of patience and a cheap digital camera.

That being said, you need to be aware there are some factors that can cause quite spectacular pictures of what seem to be orbs or related phenomena but are not.

These factors fall into three broad categories: The first is stray objects that accidentally fall into the view of the camera lens, such as stray strands of the photographer's hair or camera straps getting in front of the viewfinder.

The second is atmospheric elements that can produce orb or plasma-like images when photographed (for example, smoke from a chimney, pipe, or cigarette; your own frosty breath on a cold day or night; mist; fog; or tiny flying insects that are caught in the flash). The remedy for this sort of thing is nothing more elaborate than taking appropriate care.

The third is technical problems with the camera lens and CCD that can cause the appearance of "false" orbs. The most common problem is "lens flare," which happens when light comes into the camera lens that is not part of the image being photographed. Instead it reflects back and forth on the internal surfaces of the lens any number of times before it reaches the digital sensor. These reflections can produce very impressive circular or orb-like forms on the picture receiver. These images are usually ordered in a line across the picture. It is also noteworthy that the shapes of the orb-like elements that appear match the shape of the aperture of the lens. For example, if the camera shutter is made up of five or six elements, the fake orb image will likely have a five- or six-sided shape, very similar to the pattern caused by recording the emission of fluorescence.

The fourth factor that can produce false orb images is *bokeh*, a Japanese word meaning "blur." Photographers value the added effect that out-of-focus areas in a picture can contribute by emphasizing the central components of the picture and de-emphasizing the background. However, in the out-of-focus areas any significant point of light can become converted into a disc shape that is easily confused with an orb image.

The remedy for lens flare or *bokeh* problems is to take care where the camera is positioned relative to potentially troubling bright light sources. Watch for the characteristic concentric circle markings that characterize most genuine orbs. These concentric circles may well be due to light photons from the flash or from the surrounding areas in areas of high surplus electrons impinging on different levels of the orbs. This could cause them to fluoresce separately, thus conveying the impression of circles and also giving the orbs a flat appearance instead of spherical. It may also account for the fact that the orbs always seem to face their "front" toward the camera.

A lot of people assert that these orb and plasmoid images appear because the flash reflects off moisture, pollen, or dust particles in the air; or because of marks on the camera lens; or because of lens flare caused by light reflecting off even numbers of internal surfaces within the lens; and so on. If that were the sole reason for why the orbs are there, then it should be possible to demonstrate identical effects repeated in successive pictures. There is no doubt at all that errors of this kind can readily happen, but with care they can be avoided, and anybody who has any reasonable experience in orb photography can easily learn to spot what effects might come from moisture or precipitation, or dust or pollen particles, and what does not. But it would be absurd even at this stage of the evidence to suggest such errors could explain away the orb phenomenon.

Likewise, if you place a drop of water directly on the camera lens it is very easy to see how it causes areas to be blurred in the picture. This experiment is best done in daylight. Water droplets on the lens will not normally be able to produce a reflection of the flash back into the camera lens unless the positioning of the lens and flash relative to each other is highly unusual, and I know of no camera that has this arrangement. Presumably camera manufacturers avoid such positioning because that sort of position of lens and flash would make the taking of everyday flash pictures of acceptable quality next to impossible.

If, as some have suggested, orbs are produced by an object outside the camera reflecting light from the flash into the camera lens, which is in turn reflected back against the rear surface of the lens by the shutter, producing an image of the lens itself, then it should be possible to repeat the experiment and obtain identical results. If the shutter were to produce such a reflection it would have to be at least partially closed, which would mean the degree of exposure of the alleged "orb" would be less than the remaining part of the picture. Yet orb images are normally just as defined as other areas of the picture. If these "mechanical" explanations can account for the orb phenomenon, then it should be possible to obtain similar results by taking successive pictures in near identical conditions. As far as I am aware, this has not been done.

When a series of photographs is taken in close succession with the same camera, under the same atmospheric conditions, orb phenomena are often not found in all of the pictures in the series. This happens in pictures taken at intervals of about ten seconds apart, the time needed for the camera to "recycle": Orbs appear in the first picture, none or very few are in the second picture, and a large number of orbs appear again in the third picture. To have atmospheric conditions of such variation within a total time of thirty seconds is simply not feasible, so this factor alone is quite sufficient to show that genuine orb pictures are not due to atmospheric pollution. I have a large number of such sequences recorded on camera that shows this.

If a number of people are taking pictures at the same time and in the same location, some will obtain photographs of orbs at times, but not at other times, regardless of whether they're using film or digital cameras. Film processing errors can hardly account for the phenomena either, especially if the film is processed at different places and yet the same so-called "errors" still show up.

There cannot be film processing errors in digital cameras. In any case, when processing errors *do* take place due to a fault in the camera itself, these errors are usually square, not orb shaped, and they could not produce the semitransparent effects that have been seen, as the pixels themselves would have to be corrupted.

I have taken thousands of photos of raindrops without any orbs present in the pictures, and many more when there were. It takes very little skill or practical experience to be able to know the difference. The motion of the orbs can be contrary to the movement of the raindrops or take place in the same direction as the raindrops, or in a thousand variations between the two. I have done the same experiments with dust particles and arrived at substantially the same conclusions.

Orbs and Our Place in the Cosmos

The study of the orb phenomenon is as yet only in its infancy, so it is far indeed from the time for definite conclusions. The pictures in this book were selected from a collection of more than one hundred thousand images, most of which are of at least equal interest to the ones included here. They were taken in all sorts of conditions and the dates and times they were taken are recorded. The images have not been faked. Some were auto-balanced or had portions enlarged for better visibility, but other than that the images have been left as they were when taken. This can be verified from the images' EXIF files. It is my hope that anyone who has a digital camera and the time and patience to devote to this work will eventually be able to capture the same types of images. At that point one can make up one's own mind about the evidence.

To sum up my investigations so far:

- A careful analysis of the data collected in this study clearly shows that the orb phenomenon is real and cannot be explained away by the myriad suggestions that have been produced to account for it, such as raindrops or fog, dust particles or pollen in the air, lens flare, *bokeh*, or digital processing errors.

- The hexagonal forms that the orbs sometimes assumed gave me the clue that their images are not due to the light from the camera flash being reflected back to the camera, as is the case in ordinary photography. The orbs must generate a light from within themselves. This light most likely comes from the process of fluorescence triggered by the photons from the camera flash, which can also be aided by an abundance of free electrons in the atmosphere as can occur in rainfall or with the use of an ionizing apparatus or strobe.

- This means that the types of orbs which appear in these conditions must be electromagnetic in nature. The color of the ionizing radiation that they emit is most likely an indication of the existence of the frequencies to which they belong.

- This investigation indicates proof on the physical level that these are not simply "frequencies" but realms of existence as solid within themselves as our "physical" reality is to us.

- If this is correct then it must be asked whether we have physical proof that these orb entities, if they are not beings of the physical universe we inhabit, actually belong to other realms above this one.

- Only a minority of orbs can be equated with what ghost hunters and some religious believers identify with the spirits of the dead, so a study of the orbs from that perspective is a very limiting one.

- Our religious and cultural background poorly prepares us for an objective assessment of the implications of these phenomena regarding our place in the realms of all that exist and our destinies both before birth and after death.

- The development of what seems to be a torsion vortex (and what may be related to electromagnetic spin) in many of my orb photographs may indicate that there are most likely orb forms which are therefore not electromagnetic in nature but belong to a torsion field. The known effects of the torsion vortex on the shielding of gravity and bending of the time-space fabric will be central to a deeper understanding of this new reality.

- I've offered some practical hints on the technological side of orb photography to help in distinguishing true and false orb images. Avoiding modern digital cameras that use hot mirrors to filter out infrared radiation will help facilitate orb investigations. The photographs in this book were, however, taken with various cameras, all of which had hot mirrors installed. Digital cameras are by far preferable to film cameras for orb photography because the digital camera CCD is to some degree sensitive to spectra outside the visible range, whereas ordinary film is usually not sensitive to any significant degree.

- Only when orbs gather a sufficient collection of free electrons to themselves do they become visible to the camera; when that collection reaches a sufficient density they can also become temporarily visible to the naked eye. They can also gravitate

toward high electromagnetic fields of energy and when sufficiently charged can be detected by a simple gauss meter.

- Orbs can move their electrons around, and that may have to
do with how they are able to move. In some pictures of orbs
in flight the leading edge exhibits a blue-hued light, while the
trailing edge radiates in a brown-orange tint. If you relate that
back to the material on the significance of the light spectrum
colors it will be the basis for many interesting hypotheses.

- It is reasonable to assume that the unfolding of many different
types of orbs and orb phenomena will continue. It is equally
likely that some form of communication will develop with time.

- To say that on the basis of these investigations that one knows
all the types of orb entities that exist would be as foolish as
believing one knows all the types of people in the world simply because you are familiar with the types in your own town.

Even if those of closed mind drop the idea that this earth is
located in prime real estate in this galaxy, they nevertheless maintain
that it is still at the center of everything in "some other" way. Our
problem is not the beliefs we espouse but the arrogance that assumes
we must always be at the center of significance, even when the facts
are blatantly against it. This attitude can generate any number of
convictions that have no apparent proof.

What is at the basis of this supposed "other way"? Does it rest on
the innate superiority of the beings that make up the human race to
every other being? If so, then it is easy to see why the suggestion that
there might be intelligent life elsewhere—either in this physical uni-

verse or in the realms of higher frequency—is profoundly unsettling to people of that mind-set. The primary consequences of this are felt first not in religion but in technology and politics. Perhaps we do not sit on top of a heap of a fairly bad lot in this dimension of the physical after all. The realm of the invisible has long emerged from being the preserve of mystics and visionaries. Out of the invisible comes TV and radio programs, microwaves, cell phones, devastating nuclear radiation, and weapons guidance systems. We are no longer so blind and deaf as to imagine that what we cannot see and hear is irrelevant to us. We have come to understand that what is seen and unseen has far more to do with the limited capabilities of our senses, which evolved to provide us with an excellent middle-of-the-road perception system so that we could function in this world. These realities so ignorantly labeled as "the paranormal" and "the mystical" seem to be different simply because we cannot see and hear them. Our senses are organs of perception; they are not arbiters of what is real.

But we now realize that the realm of the paranormal and the mystical are not really different realities, any more than the fact that a horse is color-blind means that red and green are categories of an alien world. The orb phenomenon is a threat to the diehard convictions on which we have based a very false and limited estimate of our place in God's creation. It is time to tease out its implications, not to make ourselves more limited and humble, but to open up to the immense possibilities that new realities are beginning to unfold about our place and significance in the cosmos.

What seems to frighten us most is not the thought that we might be alone but that we might *not* be. And the companion fear is that what really terrifies us is not our weakness, limitations, and inability to cope but the greatness that we suspect lies hidden just beneath the surface of what we are. Most of the great thinkers in human history have known how fearful we are of the responsibility that comes with realizing we create our own destiny. The killing of the messengers that often went with this message is ample proof of how right they were. We should be under no illusions that the orb phenomenon may stir up both of these deep atavistic fears once again.

In studying orbs, while we are definitely talking of realities that are in this world, they are not physical in any customary sense. So our main difficulty in this study is likely not to be the effort to regard them as at least on the same level as us humans, but the struggle to refrain from seeing them as supernatural.

Part II

Orbs—Evidence of Divine Presence?

by

Klaus Heinemann, Ph.D.

Acknowledgments

My wife, Gundi, deserves sincere thanks for her relentless cooperation and for taking many of the pictures presented in this section. I am indebted to the Reverend Ron Roth for inviting me to take photographs during his intensives/seminars. I have also greatly appreciated numerous stimulating discussions with Dana Duryea, who contributed several pictures (figures II-18 and II-37) and valuable insights, specifically to the section "Dark Energies: Low-evolved Spirits" in chapter 10. For the photographs they contributed, I am grateful to Art and Carol Schreur (figure II-17) and my daughter Connie (figures II-8, II-9, and II-27). I thank numerous individuals for supporting my work by sending me phenomena pictures they took but that, for various reasons, did not find their way into this book.

Most important, I am grateful for the divine guidance that led me to these photographs that exhibit emanations from Spirit beings and the explanations and conclusions drawn from them.

Introduction

We Are Surrounded by a Cloud of Witnesses

My wife and I had just arrived at our favorite vacation spot on the Northern California coast. The weather was beautiful, the air fresh and cool. I had set up my laptop and was ready to add the finishing touches to this manuscript. But it wouldn't turn out that way, at least not for several days.

A few days before we left for this ten-day retreat, I received a phone call from the renowned modern-day mystic, healer, and avatar Ron Roth, telling me I should watch the television show *Ghost Hunters*. It would "deal with some aspects of spirits that should be included in the manuscript" he knew I was writing. "Without that, the book is incomplete," he said.

I had already heard of that series and had actually seen an episode or two. They had not captured my interest at all. I was able to see another episode that same evening and found it equally uninspiring. But then, that night, I was reminded of some pictures my friend Dana Duryea had sent me several weeks ago.

Dana and his group had done exactly the kind of "ghost hunting" as the people on the show, the only difference being that the aspect of sensationalism was missing. For him, this was real, "normal" work, just as teaching a class of sixth-graders or spending a day at the office might be. They were hired by the caretakers of a historic building in Southern California that was haunted by unfriendly spirits. The pictures, he stated, showed a few of the top-level spirits causing the haunting. He asked me to do some computer contrast enhancement work on the photographs to use in his report for his clients. I did so, and it was quite apparent that the photographic evidence of these dark spirits exhibited them as small *dark* disks, rather than as *light* images, as all my other pictures of Spirit emanations from evolved, "good" Spirits had looked like. (See "Dark Energies: Low-evolved Spirits" in chapter 10 for more on dark energies.)

When I had finished those digital enhancements, I considered the results not too interesting, and I had entirely discarded them for the context of this book. But after watching that evening's episode of *Ghost Hunters*, the photographs' importance became evident to me: Dark spirits appear to use quite a different mechanism to make themselves visible—or not visible, as the case may be—in photographs. They do not *emit* light but *absorb* light energy.

Then, on the day we left for our vacation, two books arrived from Ron Roth. They were heavily marked up, and in a brief note he suggested I might want to study them. I added the books to our luggage, and off we went.

When I had unpacked my computer and was ready to work on the manuscript, these two books, along with other reading material Ron had suggested, grabbed my attention, and the book editing project was set aside. I started with the voluminous book by José Lacerda de Azevedo, *Spirit and Matter: New Horizons for Medicine*. The author, a medical doctor trained and working in Brazil, recounted his experiences over several decades releasing spirit attachments and healing spirit-possessed patients.

I ended up reading the book from cover to cover, not because I was fascinated by its contents, but because the focus on harmful spirits bewildered me and I was grasping for clues that would alleviate my increasing anxiety. I found myself much more confused about Spirit emanations than before I had started. The book was reminiscent of the work of the famous nineteenth-century French spiritualist Allan Kardec, whose prayers are still used today, predominantly in Brazil and the Philippines, to invoke ancestral spirits; and of Luiz Xavier's book *The Astral City*, which describes, in incredible detail, the multilayered structure of nonphysical life around us. The "other" reality described in these books was nowhere as encouraging as my experience with orbs, which I had come to know as positive, essentially divine beings that have nothing but the best intentions for us humans in our physical reality.

I felt incapacitated. The manuscript I was about to complete seemed such a contrast to what I had just read that I was unable to concentrate on it. While I was writing with an emphasis on the *privilege* underlying the circumstance that highly evolved Spirits are making their presence around us known, Lacerda was largely reporting about how *devastating* spirits can be for us. I came away from his book with a deep doubt if mine would be beneficial for the reader.

To ease my anxiety, I meditated on the wisdom that we as "normal" human beings do not usually have *direct* awareness of the mere *existence* of the Spirit world that is all around us. How incredibly ingenious it is that we are designed to live life and acquire consciousness through becoming loving human beings, *without ever really knowing exactly where we come from and where we are going!* How superb is the wisdom of Creator! By not giving us direct, *scientifically reproducible* insight into divine reality, He/She/It gives us the opportunity to freely decide for the good and thus become truly *conscious*.

On the seventh day of our retreat I received an unusual e-mail. It was from my daughter who lives in Southern California and works as an elementary school teacher. While she was skeptical about the subject of Spirit emanation imaging I had been so fascinated with for the past couple of years, she sent me a few photos she had just taken at a school theater performance. The photos exhibited several high-contrast light beings around the children. "Check this out—*pretty amazing!*" was her comment.

This simple message put everything back in perspective: yes, even though there are some misguided dark spirits that every so often try to grab our attention, we are indeed surrounded by a cloud of highly evolved Spirit beings that are there to help us, to inspire us, to lead us on our path through the myriad challenges presented to us every day of our lives in this physical reality. They are there for no other purpose but to be of constructive assistance to us in every situation of life, from making decisions to keeping us healthy and steering us away from harm's way. *Pretty amazing*, indeed! Spirit emanations give us a wonderful assurance that we are not alone, that we are here for a purpose, that our paths have significance in the grand scheme, and that the Spirit world is actually desperately interested in us and wants us to do with our lives the very best of what we are designed to do.

Just as good and evil coexist in our physical reality, highly evolved (good) and less highly evolved (dark or evil) Spirits coexist in the Spirit world. Dwelling on the inferior ones will not move us ahead. Instead, our challenge is to empower the positive forces in both realities.

My Introduction to Spirit Emanations

Even as recently as a few years ago, had someone claimed that he had *photographed Spirits*, I would have reacted with anything from an expression of polite disbelief to a flat-out dismissal. My skepticism would have been even stronger if the person had told me that he had *identified* these images and that they were emanations from certain specific saints and other highly evolved Spirit entities.

Many people have absolutely no problem believing in such "stories." Others experience an instant blocking reaction when confronted with anecdotes that do not fit in their conditioned paradigm. Foremost among these may well rank those, like myself, whose paradigm was reinforced through formal education in the engineering sciences. It takes *hard proof* for us to shift our thinking.

Having gone through university training in experimental physics, as well as many years of research and teaching in the general area of surface physics and surface chemistry, using sophisticated techniques such as electron spectroscopy and ultra-high vacuum electron microscopy to detect details down to the atomic level of optical resolution, I have previously had—and published—insights regarding the world beyond the physical. I had joined the ranks of those scientists who profess that there is more to existence than what we can see, touch, smell, hear, measure, and calculate with our state-of-the-art scientific means.

However, it is difficult to shed one's own shadow, and for many years my preoccupation has been to reconcile my acquired belief system, which had moved far beyond the confines of the physical reality, with what the laws of the physical universe tell me *can* and *cannot* be. My books *Consciousness or Entropy?* and *Expanding Perception* in particular were attempts at bridging that gap.

My first experience with photographing orbs occurred on September 26, 2004. For me, it was a huge step in establishing *clear physical evidence of the existence of the nonphysical realm.*

I offer this work to those who, deep in their hearts, know about their place in the scheme of evolving creation but who wish for more concrete evidence to give them reassurance that their hearts are on the right track.

Actual demonstration of Spirit emanations, *proof* that they exist—going beyond what skeptics would call anecdotal evidence—has not been shown, at least not with the certainty that would persuade the typical natural scientist (physicist, chemist, engineer).[1] I wish to present some facts that have satisfied my personal thirst for "proof" that what I have long believed in is indeed irrefutable scientific evidence.

The following chapters contain, with few exceptions that are clearly noted, only pictures I have taken or witnessed myself, using several high-quality, state-of-the-art digital cameras under experimental conditions that I can justify as technically/scientifically sound.

1. There are noteworthy exceptions to this blunt statement, including the excellent work of Harvey Martin, who followed up on Dr. Berthold Schwartz's experiments in the 1980s to prove that *intelligent nonphysical beings* performed certain physical tasks. They were performed *inside* a *hermetically sealed* glass container (a fish tank) and recorded from the outside with a film camera. Recording was started when physical movement was detected inside the tank, while making sure that no outer influences,

These pictures are not diffraction phenomena of dust particles or droplets or atmospheric mist or other disturbances of any kind. They are not due to camera lens aberrations or electronic disturbances. They are real, physical representations of the objects photographed.

The pages ahead delve into the world of highly evolved Spirit beings. Let's tune in to their message!

—Klaus Heinemann

such as mechanical vibrations, temperature and humidity changes, light, or other forces could cause the movement. The phenomena photographed included such bizarre occurrences as picking up a pen inside the tank, writing a message on a piece of paper, placing it in a stamped envelope, addressing the envelope, removing the envelope from the hermetically sealed environment, and mailing it through the U.S. postal system to the addressee.

8

The Evidence

Orbs versus Spirit Emanations

The features that became the subject of this book are commonly called "orbs." However, I often refer to them using the more verbose *images of Spirit emanations*. The reason for using this unconventional description is based on the conclusions I have drawn from my research. Knowing what I know now, the word *orb* simply appears too generic and too irreverent to me. It is as if I talked about members of royalty as "John" or "Jack," or about wisdom teachings as "anecdotes."

The word *emanation* has the Latin root *ex mano*, literally meaning "from the hand" or coming "out of the hand." The meaning of the word has evolved to "something that issues from a source; an emission," "the act of coming (or going) out; becoming apparent." Either of these definitions describes quite pointedly the meaning of the word as I intend it.

So what is a Spirit emanation? What is emanating, from what is it emanating, and to what extent is that which is emanating a true reflection of that which it is emanating from? I will get into the details of my answers to these questions in chapter 10. Now, however, I want to describe a simple metaphor that can help you understand the difference between images of *Spirits* and images of *Spirit emanations*.

Imagine yourself in an airplane, late at night, in perfectly clear weather, looking out of the window into the completely dark landscape below. You happen to notice a few slowly moving lights. They seem to be moving along a line that you cannot see. Some are traveling in one direction, others in the opposite direction. Instantly you make the association that these are cars on a highway below. And instantly you make the association that these cars are driven by people like yourself. You perhaps wonder who they are and what they are thinking.

But what if you had never seen an automobile before? Say you had grown up somewhere in the jungle and had lived your entire life there. And then someone had come to your village, blindfolded you, taken you on an airplane, and lifted your blindfold after nightfall while you were still in flight. What would you have concluded then, looking out of the window and seeing those small sets of moving lights? Given the complete darkness, you likely would have concluded that there are beings out there that are entirely different from you, that, in fact, look like pairs of moving bright lights.

Obviously, one major part of your conclusion would be right on: Yes, there are indeed other beings down there. But the second part of your conclusion would be entirely wrong. The physical body of the beings down there is quite different from the white circles of lights that is *emanating* from them—or, of course, from their vehicle. The lights are not the beings, but they come from—*emanate from*—beings. They are guided by them, controlled by them, moving in patterns that originate with the will of the beings, but by no means do the circles of light describe the entirety of those beings!

The conclusion we can draw from this metaphor to our situation regarding photographing the orb phenomena is that calling those sets of lights "beings" would substantially miss the mark. Calling them "emanations from beings" would be a much more appropriate description. Similarly, calling an orb a "Spirit being" would miss the mark, but calling it an "emanation from a Spirit being" would be much more to the point.

It is, however, important to realize that not every feature in the photographs that looks like an orb is an emanation from a Spirit being. Images of droplets or microparticles suspended in the air close to the camera lens (within a few inches) can, in fact, look very similar to those of Spirit emanations. We must be discerning when we interpret such images. In the section "Addressing the Skeptic" in chapter 9, I point out differences between Spirit emanations and such simple, mundane diffraction/reflection images. I will highlight circumstances which prove that we are seeing *genuine* images of Spirit emanations and not meaningless optical effects. As we will see, such circumstances include

- Eclipsing the image by an object located between the orb and the camera
- Evidence of the orb's high-speed motion during the exposure
- Nonsymmetrical interior features of the orb image

- Sequential photos showing the *same* orb at different sizes, locations, and/or rotations
- Images of the same orb taken with different cameras from the same and different locations and angles
- Simultaneous ("stereo") images taken with two cameras

These chapters concentrate on images of Spirit emanations and the meaning behind such images. I do not present a compilation of arguments that a particular image is, in fact, an image of a Spirit being or an emanation from it. Such a proof is not the *primary* intent but rather of *secondary* concern. Therefore, I have selected for this section only pictures taken under known, controlled photographic conditions and circumstances, where I feel confident that one can rule out nonauthentic orb-*like* features at the onset. For this reason, I have chosen mostly photos taken by myself, my wife, or close friends at occasions where I was present. To underline the authenticity of the phenomena being presented, I am explicit about the experimental circumstances under which all the photos were taken.

How It All Began

The first orb photographs I have ever taken (figure II-1) were from a "Healing Prayer Intensive" seminar with the Rev. Ron Roth on September 26, 2004, in a hotel ballroom near Chicago, Illinois.[1] The

---

1. I used a Pentax Optio 330 digital camera (3.34 megapixels) in the wide angle imaging mode (7.6 mm focal length, equivalent to 40mm focal length with a standard 35-mm camera), using the built-in flash; 2048x1536x24b jpeg image resolution, 1.05 megabytes image recording.

scene is at the front stage of a large ballroom.[2] The backdrop was a dark-colored wall. A wooden equilateral triangle with a side length of approximately eighteen inches was suspended about two feet away from the wall above a table with religious insignia; the person depicted in the photograph was standing close to the table.

Note the circular feature in the upper corner of the triangle in figure 1a and the extremely bright circular feature above the head of the person in figure 1b. The latter is not a lightbulb or a light source of any kind. In a series of well over ten pictures taken at this particular event within a time span of about ten minutes, this particular feature appeared only once. Nobody in the audience had noticed it, and neither had I when I took the photograph.

When I downloaded my pictures into my computer that evening, I discovered this bright disk and was dumbfounded. Given the stunning brightness, it was quite understandable that I noticed it immediately. This is the first image of this kind I had ever seen. It is also the brightest orb I have ever photographed, even though quite a number of bright orbs would follow in the ensuing months.

My first reaction was disbelief and skepticism. I tried everything to argue it away. I went back to the ballroom to see what was really there. I found no evidence of a light source at that location. Any sort of reflection from any other light source could definitely be ruled out. My camera was in top shape. In the multitude of pictures I had taken

2. The ballroom had an approximately square footprint and was sized to hold about 600 people; approximately 250 people were in attendance. One entire side of the ballroom, to the left of the camera, consisted of windows providing a significant amount of daylight. Ceiling height was standard for modern, large ballrooms; air quality was in accordance with A/C standards. There was no smoking in the room during the intensive and at least twenty-four hours prior to the event.

within a short time before and after this one, from the very same location, none showed this high-intensity feature, which ruled out any camera defect or other optical abnormalities.

After examining many more pictures I took that day, and finding similar, equally unexplainable features in several of them, I began to realize that I was on to something *real*. These pictures exhibited features that were of a physical nature such that they could be captured with a digital camera, yet I had not noticed them with my bare eye, and there was no plausible explanation for them that would satisfy me from a scientific point of view.

This discovery prompted an intensive study of such phenomena that culminated in this book section. I did what the scientific process would suggest: look into what has already been written/published about the phenomena, devise a program to demonstrate reproducibility of the observations, determine the experimental parameters under which the effect can be observed, attempt to come up with plausible explanations, and draw conclusions from what I learned.

I also went back to well over one thousand digital pictures I had taken at previous spiritual events and, now that I knew what to look for, was able to identify a number of similar features that had previously simply escaped my attention. Some of these are presented in the following chapters. Since that first orb experience, the frequency of orb features in my pictures has skyrocketed, from on average one in about fifty pictures taken in 2002 to several *in each picture* taken now at similar occasions—a hundred-fold increase!

Being now convinced that the features I have photographed are emanations from highly conscious Spirits made me wonder about the real reason why the first one I saw was the brightest I have ever recorded. I do not think this occurred by serendipity. I believe that in the world of Spirits, there are no accidents; there are no disjointed coincidences. I believe it happened because "they" *wanted* to get my attention. They knew that I was ready to deal with what I was about to see. I had come to the point in my life when I would no longer discard this kind of a phenomenon as nonsense but, instead, would give it the benefit of the doubt and make an honest attempt to come up with an explanation that was not slanted by my scientific skepticism. A good friend and deeply spiritual, clairvoyant person (in fact, it is the person in figure II-1) offered this explanation: "They wanted to be photographed; they knew that the time was right for people to see that they are [for] real!" In her book *Prophecy*, the psychic and spiritual teacher Sylvia Browne corroborates this suggestion by flatly stating that the frequency of orb sightings has "recently greatly increased."

Since my first experience with orbs, I have photographed thousands more of them, which has taught me a great deal about the conditions and camera settings most favorable for seeing them. Let's look at those factors now.

Basic Requirements for Photographing Spirit Emanations

Flash and mobility

I noticed that images of Spirit emanations appeared only in photos taken with flash. Even when I took the photograph in broad daylight, only under certain circumstances would Spirit beings appear. In all such cases it turned out that I had used a flash to lighten up the faces of the people being photographed. (Nevertheless, the ingenuity of Spirit beings may well be so great that people might begin seeing them even without the aid of a flash.)

Since the actual duration of an electronic flash is only approximately 1/1000th of a second, it became clear that Spirits were capable of moving at a very high speed and *would do so as their normal mode of being present*. Their "standard condition" or "resting position" would not be characterized by *absence* of motion, as one might expect from comparison with physical beings, but rather by a state of super-high-speed motion. Regular photographic exposure times of, say, 1/60th of a second would normally not give a clear image of them, because at their speed they would be displaced too far during the actual exposure period and, at best, one would see only a faint streak in the picture. Such streaks, I reckoned, even if they were in the image, would be so unobtrusive that it would be hard to distinguish them from any other, "normal" features in the image. (We will pick up the subject of the flash's role in a later chapter.)

Mobility

High velocity or mobility of these features would also explain why they cannot normally be seen with the bare eye. The human eye is capable of perceiving images as separate events only if the image frames are approximately 1/20th of a second or longer apart. If the intervals of subsequent images become shorter, we tend not to see that the pictures are separate events but perceive them as continuous "motion" pictures.[3] We can infer that very fast-moving objects would escape the attention of someone with normal human visual capacity.[4]

The orb photographed in figure II-2 was at rest at the beginning of the exposure, then moved about 8 cm (3 inches), and then was again at rest at the end of the exposure. Given that everything happened within an exposure time of 1/1000th of a second, one can simply calculate that it must have moved at a velocity of least 300 km/h (200 mph)—and probably much faster!

An even faster mobility is evidenced in the bright Spirit being shown in figure II-10. In this case, the Spirit being is shown to have moved in three steps during the exposure period. It rested for a brief moment, then moved on to a new position a few inches away, where it rested again for a brief moment, only to once again move to a third position and rest there for the remainder of the exposure period—and all this within 1/1,000th of a second. If one does the simple math for this triple motion, the orb's speed must have been in excess of 500 mph.

As I will explain more fully in a later chapter, even exposure times as short as 1/1000th of a second are too long to capture Spirit emanations when they move about as they would *normally* do. In order to be photographed, they actually have to be still *intentionally*, at

3. I have spoken with several clairvoyant people who can see Spirit entities. For them, the transition from perceiving individual to motion-type pictures is typically at much shorter intervals. These people often complain that television or movie theater pictures (which contain as many as sixty [half-] frames per second) cause them headaches because of the excessive "flickering."

4. This inability of the human eye to perceive images of very short duration (less than about 1/30th of a second) is actually being experimented with in the advertising industry. Single-image frames of an advertising slogan are interspersed in a regular television feature presentation in the hopes that the viewer will subconsciously perceive the ads without consciously noticing them.

least for the short duration of the photographic exposure. Later I will demonstrate that it is possible to *request* these Spirits to *hold still* during the duration of the image exposure and that such requests can find a positive response. Not only would they hold still for me upon request, they would also beam their light in a very directed form into the camera.

Of course, when we talk about motion, we are making very simplistic assumptions about highly complex phenomena. We have inferred that the displacement from one to the next location occurs in a smooth, linear fashion. This may not at all be the case. What we are seeing may well be the positions before and after *instantaneous relocations* ("quantum jumps"). There can be successive spontaneous manifestations of nonlinear energy concentrations, happening astonishingly at physical locations that are very close to each other, such as to give the viewer—who is subject to physical constraints and would otherwise not be able to detect them—the *impression* that the motion occurred in a fast, linear fashion.

However, despite this uncertainty, one can conclude that the mere evidence of distinct motion, such as shown in figures II-2 and II-10, is proof that these orbs are not photographic defects or abnormalities, or diffraction phenomena of any kind. We will pick up this subject in chapter 9 in the section "General Indicators for Authenticity."

Camera type

I took most pictures with either a Pentax Optio 330 digital camera (3.34 megapixels resolution; see footnote 1) or a state-of-the-art Nikon Coolpix 8800 (2005) digital camera with 8 megapixel resolution. In both cases, I used the highest resolution mode, which yielded pictures of about 1 to 1.5 megabytes with the Pentax and 4 to 6 megabytes with the Nikon camera. I reduced the picture size only after image processing and fitting for publication and printing, assuring that no significant evidence of the features I intended to show was lost in the size reduction process and no errors of any kind were introduced due to reduced image quality.

I noticed no difference between the results obtained with either camera, except that, as one would expect, the higher resolution capability of the Nikon camera revealed more details of the *interior* features of the Spirit emanation images and allowed higher detail magnifications, which was particularly useful when the Spirit emanation images were small (i.e., when they were in a more contracted mode).

I have also evaluated numerous pictures sent to me by other people who knew that I was interested in orb images. These pictures were taken with a wide spectrum of cameras and under unknown experimental conditions. Even though many had inferior resolution or were taken at an inferior resolution setting, there appeared to be no evidence that would relate the frequency of capturing Spirit emanations to the type or model of the camera used.

Photographic Enhancement

Contrast enhancement
Figure II-1a reveals that there is a low-contrast image of a Spirit in front of the upper corner of the triangle. Figure II-3 shows an

enlarged segment of that picture. I applied straightforward electronic image enhancement to the picture, as is available with standard commercial software.[5] *Increasing* the gamma and *decreasing* the contrast settings resulted in figure II-3. Such image enhancement is scientifically legitimate in that it does not compromise the interpretation as an authentic image, because it is applied *uniformly* to the entire photograph and does not introduce new information—it only indiscriminately enhances certain already existing image information. This is quite comparable to what conventional photographers would accomplish with filters.[6]

Color enhancement

Depending on the type of Spirit emanation being photographed, as well as on other photographic conditions, such as the background color, the most productive method of electronic image enhancement can be *color* enhancement rather than contrast enhancement. An example is shown in figure II-5, which depicts another scene taken on September 26, 2004, at the same seminar. The scene of this photo is a few feet farther to the left on the stage of the ballroom than that of figure II-1 (see footnote 2 for more specifics on conditions).

Rev. Roth is performing a healing on a severely challenged baby. The original image (top) shows only low-contrast evidence of orbs being present. Most are apparent near the head of the standing per-

5. I used ACDSee.

6. However, electronic image processing cannot be compared with "pushing" (accelerating) or "pulling" (decelerating) certain image features during old-fashioned processing of conventional film in liquid developers in a darkroom. Such manipulation is normally not applied equally to the entire picture, and I would, therefore, not consider it an acceptable method to enhance orb photographs.

son. Only a relatively minor change of the color balance introduces a dramatic change in the image. A large green orb became apparent within the dark background area on the right side.

Note that the two Spirit beings near the head of the standing woman were only little changed in contrast and color during this color enhancement process. We can conclude that the color in which emanations of Spirit beings can show up on photos varies. This means, of course, that the *wavelength/frequency spectrum* changes. Specifically, if a color sensitivity is noted, this translates to certain missing spectral wavelengths or frequencies. However, the majority of images of Spirit emanations I have observed appeared in black/white contrast and was invariant to color enhancement.

Not all images of orbs lend themselves to either contrast or color enhancement methods. For example, the Spirit image underneath the "prayer basket" (in figure II-12) and the images taken in broad daylight (figure II-11) did not yield marked visibility improvement upon either color or contrast level enhancement.

Size and Location Changes

The two images shown in figure II-4 were taken on February 4, 2003, in a large hotel ballroom. You can see part of the ceiling and the front wall of the auditorium. The exposures were taken in as rapid succession as is possible in digital flash photography (i.e., approximately five seconds apart). They show two remarkable features. First, it appears that the *same* Spirit being was photographed. This is deduced from interior features in the orbs, which are the same in both pictures, albeit somewhat rotated (e.g., the "eye," located at the outer periphery in the nine o'clock position in the upper picture, rotated to the eleven o'clock position and more inward in the lower picture). The second remarkable feature is that between the two exposures it changed size, location, and rotation. The white arrows point to a common reference point in both photographs, which attests to the change in location of the Spirit being. While the size scale in both photographs is close to the same, the diameter of the orb in the lower picture is smaller than in the upper picture, which indicates that a change in size has occurred.

I have observed this behavior numerous times with clearly different orbs. For example, figure II-6 shows a number of Spirit emanations at a lecture by author and medium Harvey Martin to an audience of about four hundred spiritual retreat participants on March 5, 2005, in Sedona, Arizona.[7] The photographs were taken a few seconds apart in the sequence shown. It appears that the Spirit emanations are "pacing" back and forth, constantly changing position and size, but each time pausing just long enough to be photographed without blurring.[8]

We can see that Spirit emanations are capable of changing their size and their location as they wish. These are remarkable character-

7. Harvey Martin is well known through his book on the Philippine Espiritistas movement. He gave this lecture on invitation by Ron Roth at one of his healing/prayer intensives.

8. The pictures in Figure II-6 were taken with a high-resolution Nikon Coolpix 8800 camera in the large ballroom of the Hilton Hotel in Sedona, Arizona. I was positioned about halfway back on the side of the room and used a mid-range telephoto setting. The table above which the Spirit being is photographed was close to a dark backdrop wall. Due to the distances involved, the backdrop appears darker than it actually was.

istics that we will pick up in the afterword, which deals with Spirit-directed healing.

Spirits Show Up at Various Occasions

Spirits do not just "attend" highly spiritual events, as the pictures in the preceding chapters might suggest. Instead, they have been observed at a wide range of occasions.

The pictures in figure II-7 were taken at a birthday party on March 6, 2005, in Sedona, Arizona, when a group of musicians performed on stage for a crowd of well over three hundred people.[9] One spirit emanation appears to have positioned itself—for just a fraction of a moment—directly on one of the musicians' hats, while another one is "hiding" behind a plant. There were Spirit emanations like these in every single one of the numerous pictures I took at this event.

Figure II-8 was taken at a performance of a fifth-grade school class on March 24, 2005, in southern California. It is one of a series of pictures exhibiting Spirit emanations present at the event. The unusually high number of photographed Spirit emanations may underline the validity of the saying, "Guardian angels are not far away—particularly from children." These pictures were taken from the very back of the auditorium (about sixty feet from the stage).[10] I had no intention and no expectation to capture Spirit emanations; my intention was only to photograph scenes of the play.

9. Same location and camera as in figure II-6.
10. I used the high-resolution Nikon Coolpix 8800 camera.

My daughter took the pictures shown in figure II-9 at a school performance at the same location a year later. The interior features of the orbs are substantially different from those photographed in the prior year, indicating that the Spirit being making its presence known this time was not the same as the one that presented itself a year earlier. The orb images shown in the two photographs of figure II-9 appear to be the same, indicating that the same spirit being can occasionally be photographed in successive images, typically at different locations, sizes, and rotational positions.[11]

Figure II-10 presents further evidence that certain Spirits love to be around children. In this particular setting, a birthday scene showing my granddaughter and my son, no fewer than ten orbs are present in the original photo. One of them is particularly bright. Upon closer examination (see enlarged image), you can see that it is triple-displaced, meaning that during the short duration of the flash, the orb moved from one position, where it rested briefly, to another, where it again rested, and then to yet another one, where it once again rested. This gives rise to a very high velocity and mobility.

The photographs in figure II-11 were taken in broad daylight at the healing center of the Brazilian healer John of God ("João de Deus," João Teixeira de Faria) in the assembly room (top) and side yard of his healing center in Abadiânia, Brazil.[12] The orbs photographed here look substantially different from those we had observed

11. The square boxes in the figure outline the positions of the orb, moving from above the heads of the children to the lower left side in the photo; the size was reduced to roughly one-half, and the new position was rotated counterclockwise by about thirty degrees.

12. The picture is cropped from a group photo; the orb appeared about six feet above the heads of the people in the group. Both photos were taken with a Pentax Optio 330 camera.

on other occasions. They are possibly evidence of a different class of Spirits, as I will explain in a subsequent chapter.

Strategic Positioning

Photographs of orbs frequently show Spirit beings positioning themselves among people or objects in such a way that we can infer a meaning.

At a Ron Roth healing intensive seminar in September 2004, a number of photographs I took show a chair in the foreground on which a basket was placed that contained hundreds of written prayer requests from the audience. In one of numerous images taken of that scene, an orb showed up and positioned itself directly underneath that basket (figure II-12). We might read into this, on the "lighter" side, that humor is not just a human quality or, on the more significant side, that our prayers are indeed treated with respect in the Spirit world. The Spirit being's positioning under the prayer basket might well have been *intended* to communicate that message to us.

Figure II-13 was taken after a worship service held by the Rev. Roth on April 8, 2006. The singer's performance had been outstanding. Her voice was magnificent—and a Spirit being seems to agree! [13]

In figure II-14, an orb is shown, in fast motion, positioned underneath the picture of the "Laughing Jesus" on the altar at the same retreat. On the left side of the altar, a large painting (30 inches × 30 inches) representing Jesus is being visited by an orb (figure II-15).

---

13. This picture was not electronically enhanced.

Figure 16 shows an example where Spirits beings "decide" to join in and make themselves visible in large numbers. The photos were taken at the beginning and at the end of a fifteen-minute speech by a high-ranking leader of the Oneness University in southern India, on invitation by Ron Roth at his spiritual retreat in Oak Brook, Illinois, in November 2005. At the beginning (left), just the "usual" number (a few) of Spirit beings was apparent; at the end (right), "crowds" of Spirits beings were present.

Huge numbers of orbs are present not only at "spiritual" events. Figure II-17 shows what happened at a mundane (albeit invitational, black-tie) wine tasting/auction event: Masses of Spirit beings crowd the space underneath the ceiling of the grand ballroom. Many pictures taken at the event in rapid succession show multitudes of orbs essentially randomly positioned.

Of course, the number of Spirit emanation images appearing in a photograph should not be taken as indicative of anything other than that these Spirits chose to make their presence known/seen in the particular photograph. It seems to me that it would be inappropriate to conclude anything like "the more, the better," as we so often do with our human mind-set. I go into more detail on this subject in chapter 10.

While it appears obvious that the Spirit emanation shown in figure II-18 at the occasion of John of God's performance of "visible" surgery at the Casa de Dom Inácio in Abadiânia, Brazil, must have had a specific reason to position itself at the neck of one of the numerous onlookers, it can only be speculated what that reason might be.[14]

14. For more on the subject of visible and invisible surgeries at the Casa de Dom Inácio, see the afterword.

The two (one large and one small) Spirits depicted in figure II-19 positioned themselves in close proximity to Ron Roth in Abadiânia, Brazil, at the occasion of a spiritual healing event in the courtyard of a *posada*. The orbs are strategically positioned in both the front and back of the Rev. Roth, as if to underline his complete protection.

There appears to be little doubt as to who is in charge of the spiritual healing event depicted in figure II-20. The photographed orb is positioned on the Rev. Roth's head.[15]

Yet another evidence of strategic positioning of a Spirit being is shown in figure II-24, where the Spirit being appears to direct the healer's arm. Note that a number of other orbs are "watching." It is interesting to point out that this picture shows a Spirit emanation that is "oddly" cut off at the end of the curtain and does not protrude into the black background, which is the opposite of what one would expect; contrast is usually enhanced, not suppressed, if the being is in front of a dark backdrop (a topic discussed in more detail in chapter 9).

Figure II-22 shows a Spirit emanation near Ron Roth while he is teaching to a large audience on March 7, 2006. A second spirit emanation is present near the video screen.[16]

15. It is actually clearly located on the side *opposite* to the camera. An object positioned between the camera and the orb is, in and by itself, clear proof of authenticity of the Spirit emanation image. It categorically rules out all arguments that a camera defect, a lens aberration, reflection, dust, or a moisture particle close to the camera may have caused the image. I discuss this important finding in chapter 9.

16. I do not believe that this is the same orb. It is a bit too small, a bit too high, and does not correlate exactly with the position of the video camera, which was at about the same height as the Rev. Roth's head. Furthermore, if it were a feature in the video, rather than a live orb, it would be expected to have an elliptical outline, commensurate with the angle under which the video screen is seen in the image.

Spirit Images in the Night Sky

Images of orbs taken in the night sky are easily prone to be false (reflections of dust particles or humidity droplets in the air) and/or identify what is known as "nature spirits." If we can assume that most of the Spirit emanations we have shown up to this point have a highly evolved nature (commensurate with the spiritual nature of the event at which they were photographed), we can equally assume that a great number of other Spirits exists that, perhaps, correspond to our animals, insects, plants, and other life forms in the physical reality.[17] These "nature spirits" would much more likely be expected outdoors than indoors.[18] Against the backdrop of a black sky, even very low-intensity—perhaps less aware or less conscious—Spirit emanations can be detected. Of the numerous pictures taken outdoors at night, I am presenting only two in this context, as Dr. Ledwith focuses heavily on orb pictures taken under these conditions in part 1 of this book.

While the scene depicted in figure II-19, which was taken out-doors at night, portends to witness the presence of highly evolved Spirits, commensurate with the evolved nature of the spiritual healing activity they are participating in, figure II-23 may include a number of nature spirits. I do, however, suggest that at least the three orbs

17. In my books *Expanding Perception* and *Consciousness or Entropy?*, I discuss the difference between the "physical" and "spiritual" realities in depth.

18. The term *nature spirits*, and their existence, is widely accepted in the literature dealing with the world of spirits. It is entirely beyond the scope of this book to even begin to get into this topic. However, if this subject interests you, I recommend the book *Spirit and Matter* by José Lacerda de Azevedo, M.D., who reports about the various levels of beings in the world of spirits in the same way as we describe civilizations in our physical world.

enlarged in the lower part of figure II-23 are highly evolved Spirits. This suggestion is corroborated by my clairvoyant consultant, who identified these three orbs as specific evolved Spirits. She also indicated that the top left mandala-like feature contains *six individual* Spirit emanations.[19]

Figure II-21 is one of several photos I took in rapid succession in front of the home of a friend in Abadiânia, Brazil, who is clairvoyant and identified the orb as the Spirit emanation of one whose presence she "had strongly felt" that evening. It showed in only one of the pictures taken. The bright spot in the center of the picture is the rising moon.

Communication with Spirits

Ever since I first realized that Spirit emanations show up in my pictures, I wondered if it was possible to entice certain Spirits to show their presence at certain locations in my picture. Since we are photographing emanations from *conscious* beings, the logic—albeit strange and unfamiliar—would be compelling to assume that there would have to be a way to communicate with those beings on simple terms.

My first attempt was simply to nonverbally express the request that, whichever Spirit beings were around, they would position themselves in a photographically opportune place and hold still long enough to be photographed without being blurred. While it is

19. The courtyard where we were seated was a grassy area, bordered by tiled walkways, and the air was clear—no moisture and no dust, but there was rain not too long before, which entirely eliminated the possibility of dust. (See "Addressing the Skeptic" in chapter 9 for a discussion of the importance of these factors.)

impossible to *objectively* prove or quantify the result of such an experiment, I can *subjectively* state that ever since I started that practice, my success rate of capturing orbs in my photographs increased at a statistically significant pace. As I mentioned earlier, since I first started taking orb pictures five years ago, I've seen a hundred-fold increase in the number of genuine orbs appearing in my pictures—under otherwise the same conditions (including the same camera used at the same type of spiritual seminar).

On June 11, 2005, I had the opportunity of going a step further. My wife and I participated in a closing event of a retreat center where we had attended many spiritual seminars over three decades, under the leadership of the center's founders, Dr. Harry and Emilia Rathbun, a remarkable couple who had been our spiritual leaders and models for as many years. They had both passed on, and the retreat center had been sold.

When we walked by one of the cabins in which we had stayed numerous times, I took the picture shown in figure II-25, the first among some fifty I took at the occasion of this "good-bye" celebration. However, there was something special about it. It was the only one for which I *specifically* requested the Spirits of our two former spiritual leaders to be present and *position themselves strategically and "hold still" during the exposure* so they would be clearly visible in this photograph. Not only did the photo yield two well-contrasted orbs, but it turned out that this was the *only one* among all the pictures I took at the event in which two large orbs clearly appeared.

I have, of course, no *irrefutable* proof that the two orbs in that picture are the Spirits of these two great teachers. However, the observation corroborates well with the observation I discuss in the section "Classifying Interior Features" in chapter 9. That examination indicates that quite frequently the same Spirit being, or group of beings, may be present around a particular person at various occasions, especially if the person is spiritually inclined. The interiors of these two images in figure II-25 are different from any of the other Spirit emanations I had ever photographed.

There is yet another facet to this already extraordinary story. After Harry had passed on in 1989, Emilia continued teaching until just a week before her passing in 2004 (at age ninety-eight). During her last two years, my wife and I had numerous meetings with her, in which we were fortunate to talk about, and learn about, her matured understanding and expectation of *Life* after life. At one of our last meetings, Emilia agreed that she would give us a sign from the other side that would help us in our own understanding of the world of the Spirits. The picture certainly ranks high among the answers we have obtained to date!

Now that I have presented some of my observations from interactions with Spirit emanations, in the next chapter we will turn our attention to analyzing the findings that have emerged from my years of photographing them.

9

Taking a Closer Look

In this chapter we'll take a closer look at orbs, at the photographic process, and at some of the substantive findings I've uncovered. In the first part of this discussion, I address the experimental conditions under which I took the pictures and which I think must prevail in order to assure that the photographs indeed show images of Spirit emanations and not photographic abnormalities. We will then look at possible categories and classifications of Spirit emanations as suggested by orb photographs.

The Photographic Process

What is really going on when we see orbs in digital photographs? What are the conditions under which we can see them, and what can we conclude from identifying these conditions?

We know that one principal condition, at least for the overwhelming majority of such images, appears to be the use of an electronic flash. We also know that using a digital camera, as compared to a conventional camera using film, is *almost* a requirement. Published works *do* exist that include orb pictures taken with conventional cameras,[1] but digital cameras are far more effective in terms of color and contrast enhancement, cost, and practicality.

The digital camera responds to information in the visible light spectrum (between approximately 300 and 800 nm wavelength). It is, therefore, logical to conclude that when we use a digital camera we are recording images of Spirit emanations predominantly in this spectral range. Furthermore, as I have shown in many of the pictures presented thus far, the vast majority of Spirit emanation images is white and does not respond to color enhancement. White light is composed of a multitude of spectral colors in correct proportion. From this we can conclude that the "object" of those images sends out light in the full, complete, *visible* color spectrum, not just at one particular wavelength. This contrasts with suggestions that orbs are images of phenomena in the infrared spectral region. However, it may well be possible that the world of Spirit beings is highly diverse, and there are so many ways of photographing orbs that, as is often the right response in spiritual matters, an "either/or" understanding should be replaced with a "both/and" attitude.

1. Leonore Sweet, *How to Photograph the Paranormal.*

The flash emits light at high color temperature that simulates white light under daytime conditions.[2]

The flash's role could be twofold:

1. It serves as a light source that creates a reflection at the object being photographed, whereby the intensity of the light coming from the object is high enough for the camera's detection.

2. It is an effective means for drastically reducing the exposure time (from typically 1/30th to 1/60th of a second for standard photography to approximately 1/1000th of a second in flash photography), making it possible to record fast-moving objects with far less blurring than would result in normal photography.

We can exclude that Spirit emanations have any physical *mass* at which "normal" light reflection (i.e., electromagnetic waves in the visible spectrum) or induced light emission could take place. The mechanisms of *reflection* or "normal" induced light emission, therefore, do not apply. We can, however, also exclude that orbs are *self*-emitting light (i.e., energy) in the visible spectrum. This would mean that you and I should be able to see them also without flash, but I am unaware of ever having produced an image of a genuine orb without using a

2. The spectrum of the flash contains many colors of the visible spectrum and peaks (in intensity) in the blue spectral range, giving a "color temperature" of upward of 5,600 degrees K (about three thousand degrees corresponds to incandescent light, 5,600 degrees to light at mid-day). Clearly, the vast majority of the photons emitted in an electronic flash are energetically higher than infrared light.

flash.[3] So there is a "clear" dilemma: We have no physical objects at which "normal" reflection can take place, and we have no light-emitting objects, but we must nevertheless rely on the flash playing a key role in the imaging process.

There are two more experimental observations that might help us understand the flash's role:

1. Color enhancement usually does not yield higher-contrast images of orbs (except for relatively rare occasions where we do see a clear color response; these occasions are discussed later in this chapter). In the majority of cases that I have observed, orbs are simply captured as white objects, regardless of color enhancement, and in those cases we must assume that the color spectrum emitted by, or reflected at, those objects contains a superposition of essentially the entire visible spectrum and does not favor infrared frequencies.[4]

2. The interior of images of Spirit emanations (discussed in detail later in this chapter) is not particularly "sharp" but resembles that of holographic images and/or contains characteristics of diffraction/interference images.

3. Even the images shown in figure II-11 were taken with the aid a flash—at the time I simply intended to "lighten up" the faces of the people photographed. Taking a photograph at a fast exposure time such as 1/1000th of a second without a flash would require very bright lighting conditions, such as in sunlit snow scenes. Since the background under such conditions would likely be of bright color, Spirit beings, if they emitted light themselves, would likely have such low contrast against that type of background that they would be extremely difficult, if not impossible, to see.

4. This occurs in an intensity distribution corresponding to a color temperature of five thousand to six thousand degrees K.

The combination of these observations cannot be explained with a simple rationale. It hints at a mechanism that is *induced* by the flash to *emit* light in the visible spectrum.

But what induces this photon emission? It would have to be expected that it is some sort of "energetic globe of plasma," which would also explain why orbs typically show up as circular images. If it is true that Spirits are able to concentrate their "energy" in physical form into physical locations as they please,[5] then it is reasonable to assume that it is possible that this energy "globe" can be excited by the visible light energy contained in the flash to emit electromagnetic energy, including in the visible light spectrum (i.e., photons or "light").

The appearance of these Spirit emanation images in a form that is somewhat reminiscent of an out-of-focus image, showing contours that look like Fresnel fringes,[6] could be rationalized as due to the spherical shape of the "plasma" globes. The strong field inside the globes could affect trajectory changes for the emitted light that would explain those fringes. In other words, light emitted at the far side of the globe would have to travel farther through the interior of the globe than light emitted at the near side. If the globe itself is of a supranatural substance, such as some sort of magneto-electric plasma,

5. There is an abundance of (albeit scientifically anecdotal) evidence of such phenomena. One example, apparitions of the Holy Mother, is discussed in greater detail in chapter 10.

6. Fresnel fringes are optical diffraction phenomena. For example, if you shine a light beam against a plate with a very small hole and record the light distribution (the "image" of the hole) on a photographic medium (or with a digital camera) behind the plate, you would not—as might be expected—get a perfect, small bright "disk" on the photograph. Instead, the edges of the disk are blurred and consist of one or more concentric rings that extend both inside the illuminated image of the hole and in the dark space around it. These are Fresnel fringes.

it is conceivable that it would bend or diffract the emitted physical light, which in turn could explain the out-of-focus appearance.

Such an explanation is, in fact, quite plausible. Given the incredibly unusual circumstance that we *are* photographing Spirit emanations, these beings can be assumed to exist in a reality that is so superior to ours that they are simply able to concentrate their energy of existence (what is equivalent to "mass" in our physical reality) in such a way that a flash's electromagnetic waves can excite energetic quantum emissions from them that are in the visible light spectrum.

However, there are many holes in this sort of explanation, which seems commensurate with the fact that we are, after all, dealing with nonphysical—albeit real—phenomena.

Extracting from this pseudo-explanation the significant and irrefutable points, we must note that we are dealing with a form of *energy*—an energy that can be detected with physical means and can thus have an effect on physical occurrences.

Addressing the Skeptic

I have already alluded to the subject of authenticity of Spirit emanations. Not all "phenomena" images do, in fact, show the phenomena one is looking for or thinking of at first glance. It is important to use discernment and distinguish the true from the false.

Figure II-26 is an example of a photograph showing features that *look like* orbs but are not genuine emanations from Spirit beings. I took it *deliberately* for the purpose of demonstrating how easy it is to "create" what looks like an astonishing image of a multitude of nature spirits. It was taken with the same high-resolution Nikon Coolpix 8800 digital camera I used for many of the other photos presented here. The only difference is that I released a fine mist of water vapor from a simple spray bottle about three to five inches away from the camera lens immediately prior to the exposure. As the camera was set for focusing on distant objects, the reflection of the flash at these droplets created out-of-focus images of the droplets that turned out to have many of the features of true Spirit emanation images.

Similar effects can be obtained if fine dust particles are near the camera, such as is shown in figure II-27. This picture was taken immediately following the completion of some demolition work in a room being prepared for remodeling. There was a great deal of dust in the air. This condition might occur in dry natural outdoor situations, particularly in rural environments, although probably not to this extent.

There are many situations where it is quite reasonable to assume that what looks like orbs was actually "created" by reflection at dust particles dispersed in the air. The effect is most prevalent in outdoor nighttime images, because the dark background enhances the contrast of these erroneous effects—along with the contrast of true Spirit emanation images that are also most readily photographed against a dark backdrop. It is, therefore, very important to use discernment when interpreting orb images taken in a dark, out-of-doors environment.

I selected the image in figure II-27 from a number of photographs taken at that occasion, because it also contains an example of an image of a (very likely) genuine Spirit emanation, "erring" amidst hundreds of "dust orbs." To arrive at that conclusion, I enlarged the outlined section in figure II-27 (shown in the lower left insert) and then color-enhanced it (lower right). The enlarged area contains an orb that appears to be in motion, which is usually a very strong indicator for authenticity as a Spirit emanation image. As you can see, this feature is significantly brighter than all other features, which are likely nothing but flash reflections at dust particles suspended in the air close to the camera lens. Furthermore, it also responds quite differently to the color enhancement process, in that its color essentially remained white, while all other orb-*like* (fake) features changed their colors. When doing color enhancement with the photographs taken from the artificial orbs caused by water droplets (figure II-26), a change of color can easily be obtained, and the color change is the same in every single droplet.

While orb-like features that show different colors upon color enhancement cannot be *categorically* ruled out as genuine images of Spirit emanations merely on the basis of their color behavior, the *difference* in color enhancement behavior of that one feature among many others in essentially the same environment *does* suggest that it is likely of a different nature. Although we cannot be entirely certain—in part also because the appearance of the feature identified as being in motion is not as clear as it would typically appear in "normal" pictures with moving Spirit emanation features (e.g., figure II-10)—it is likely that the color difference behavior is indicative that it is genuine.

Figure II-28 shows a nighttime street scene typical for third-world country conditions. I took the photo from a slow-moving car, window wide open, camera barely outside the vehicle confines, at a scene where there was quite a bit of dust in the air due to numerous vehicles moving on an extremely dusty road. I was actually *expecting* to see many orb-like reflection effects (i.e., "fake" orbs) and took the photo for the express reason to demonstrate just that. In fact, there are hundreds of them in the image, so many that they are the reason for the overall fuzziness of the picture. The lower portion of the figure shows an enlarged and slightly contrast-enhanced section of the area around the bicycle.

This is typical of a great number of such pictures taken in rural areas at nighttime, and it underlines that diligence must be taken in the analysis of orb-like features in photos taken under such conditions, to assure that what are really dust particles are not interpreted as images of Spirit emanations. This situation does happen much more frequently than you might think. I have received numerous pictures of this questionable nature from people who knew that I was interested in orbs. Many of them were night images in dusty, rural environments, and what looked like an astonishing multitude of Spirit emanation images are, most likely, nothing but reflections at dust particles.

Discerning real from fake orbs takes time, practice, and diligence. The more you photograph orbs, the more you will be able to distinguish orb-*like* features from real orbs. I suggest you experiment with color and contrast enhancements to see if some images that resemble orbs act differently than others under these conditions. Specifically, fake orbs respond more to color enhancement than authentic orbs. In the next section I describe additional indicators of authenticity.

Skeptics often argue that because a distinction between genuine orbs and simple reflection phenomena cannot *always* be made, we can only conclude that *no* images of orbs are genuine photographs of Spirit emanations. As Leonore Sweet notes, such reasoning would be as flawed as the suggestion that simply because there is a certain number of counterfeit twenty-dollar bills in circulation, the twenty-dollar note in your wallet is not worth twenty dollars. The fake and the real coexist.

General Indicators for Authenticity

Erroneous effects can essentially be ruled out if one or more of the following experimental conditions are met:

- *An object is positioned between the camera and the observed orb.* This is arguably the strongest proof of authenticity, as it—in and of itself—rules out virtually *all* arguments that can be raised by skeptics. Dust particles or droplets must be within a few inches from the camera lens to cause "fake" orb-like images; if the orb image is demonstrably far away (more than one foot) from the camera, that error is ruled out. I have numerous images of Spirit emanations that fall into this authenticity category, and you can see clear examples in figures II-7, II-20, and II-29.[7]

- *An orb is photographed in rapid motion* (such as is shown in figures II-2, II-10, II-27, and II-30), where the speed is calculated to be, at minimum, several hundred miles per hour. This is *much*

---

7. Figure II-29 was taken at a seminar led by the Rev. Ron Roth, who is seated in the foreground. Two orbs were imaged that are located *behind* the altar veil, center left, and *behind* the right flagpole, respectively. The clipped orbs are enlarged in the lower details of figure II-29.

faster than any physical dust particle or water droplet could conceivably move, even if one takes into account the increased angle velocity that would apply if the particle or droplet is close to the camera lens. The water droplets that led to figure II-26 had arguably the fastest velocity such droplets can ever attain in an atmospheric environment, yet none of the particles exhibits unidirectional blurring, as one would expect if a fast-moving object is photographed.

- *The same orb is imaged in successive image frames,* whereby it has moved between exposures from one location to another and has changed its size and orientation. This, again, is a stand-alone proof of authenticity. Good examples are shown in figures II-4 and II-9.

- *Several photos are taken from the same scene within a short time interval,* and one shows orbs while others don't, or show orbs in randomly different locations. Virtually all the pictures I present were taken under these conditions, and I have repeatedly shown such pairs of images to emphasize this point.[8] While this alone does not entirely rule out the influence of dust and moisture particles in close vicinity of the lens, it certainly does rule out other arguments of skeptics that relate to camera defects, reflections at aperture openings, and the like.

- *Orbs appear at very high image intensity.* Low-intensity orbs are typically more suspect than those that can clearly be seen without digital enhancement. Examples of extraordinarily

8. See also figure II-31. The two photos were taken about a minute apart. Very bright orbs show in different locations.

high–intensity orbs are shown in figures II-1, II-7, II-15, and II-30, as well as in figure II-31, where two scenes are shown that were photographed within a minute from left to right across the front of the ballroom. Again, no image enhancement was applied in either of these photos. The orbs are so bright that this alone all but proves authenticity.

- *Stereo image pairs show the same orb.* One might expect that images taken of the same scene at the *exact* same time with two cameras spaced laterally a few inches apart should give rise to the spatial position of an orb that happens to be imaged in both pictures. Such experiments are the subject of the next section. They give further interesting insight into the physical nature of Spirit emanations.

- *Extraordinary locations of an orb.* If an orb is located at a certain location that can be identified as truly extraordinary, such an image is very likely a genuine orb. We have, on a number of occasions, obtained images of orbs in pointed locations, such as is shown in figures II-12, II-13, and II-24.

Stereo Photography of Spirit Emanations

When we view a scene, we can typically determine without difficulty if one object is located before or behind another. Of course, one reason that we can do this is through our intellect, which tells us from our experience that, if an object appears smaller than another object that we know has the same size, it must be further away. The other reason why we can differentiate between near and distant objects is

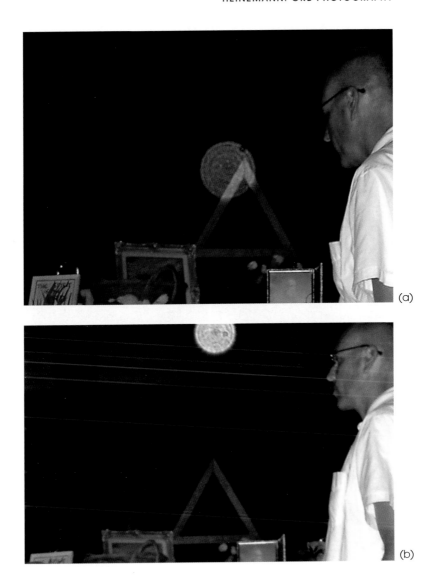

(a)

(b)

Figure II-1: Digital flash photos taken at a Spirit-directed healing seminar with Ron Roth on September 26, 2004, about a minute apart.

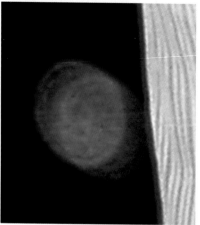

Figure II-2: Spirit being in motion. The velocity in this image is estimated at 200 mph (300 km/h). (The lower image is an enlargement from the above image.)

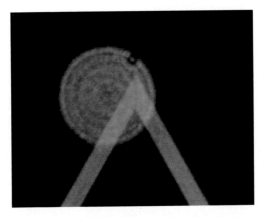

Figure II-3: Detail enlargement of the orb feature shown in figure II-1a, after electronic contrast enhancement.

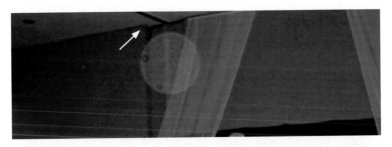

Figure II-4: Change of size and location of evidently the same Spirit being, photographed a few seconds apart at a spiritual consecration celebration on February 4, 2003. The arrow points to the same reference feature on the wall/ceiling.

Figure II-5: Color enhancement of a scene photographed on September 26, 2004; unprocessed (top) and color enhanced (bottom).

Figure II-6: "Pacing" Spirit emanations accompanying a lecturer.

Figure II-7: At a birthday party on March 6, 2005. The large orb at the lower right is behind the picture.

Figure II-8: At a fifth-grade school performance in Southern California, on March 24, 2005. Note that the intensity of the main orb is very close to the intensity of the white poster bearing the number "13."

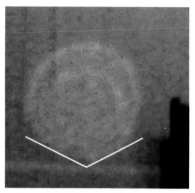

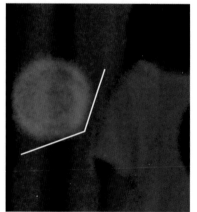

Figure II-9: Photo taken on June 8, 2006 at the same school as in figure II-8. The interior structure of the orb is quite different from the image taken a year earlier. Apparently the same orb is shown in both photos; it changed location, size, and rotation.

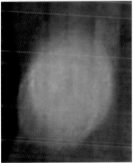

Figure II-10: No fewer than ten Spirit emanations can be counted in this scene depicting my granddaughter and my son. One of them is quite bright and exhibits triple displacement, meaning that in the short duration of the exposure, it moved and rested at three different locations.

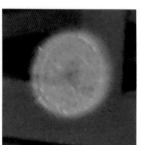

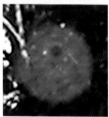

Figure II-11: At the Casa de Dom Inácio, Abadiânia, Brazil, January 24, 2004, in the main meeting hall (top) and garden (below).

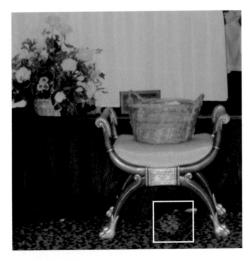

Figure II-12: A Spirit positioned itself under a "prayer basket" at a Ron Roth intensive seminar, September 26, 2004.

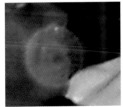

Figure II-13: The Rev. Ron Roth thanks a talented singer for her contributions to his worship service.

Figure II-14: A high-brightness Spirit emanation, in fast motion, positions itself under the picture of the "laughing Jesus" on the altar (March 7, 2006, Ron Roth retreat, Chicago).

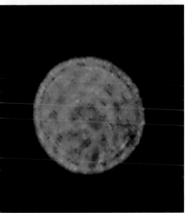

Figure II-15: A large Spirit emanation is present above a large (30 inch x 30 inch) painting representing Jesus, standing near the altar at the same retreat (March 7, 2006). Below: enlarged and contrast-enhanced.

Figure II-16: A representative of the Oneness University in the Golden City, India, at a presentation to an audience of a Ron Roth intensive seminar, November 11, 2005. At the beginning of the speech, a few Spirit emanations were visible; at the end (right) there were hundreds.

(Photo courtesy of Curt and Carol Schreur)

Figure II-17: Masses of Spirit beings are positioned under the ceiling of the grand ballroom at the occasion of a black-tie, wine-tasting event in Scottsdale, Arizona, in June 2006.

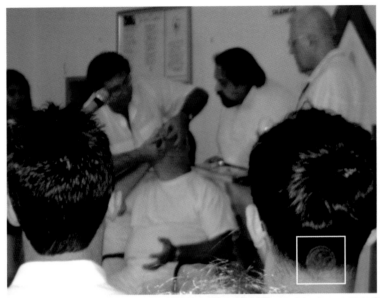

(Photo courtesy of Dana Duryea, taken in my presence)

Figure II-18: John of God performs visible surgery at the Casa de Dom Inácio in Abadiânia, Brazil, on May 20, 2005. An orb "works" on a bystander.

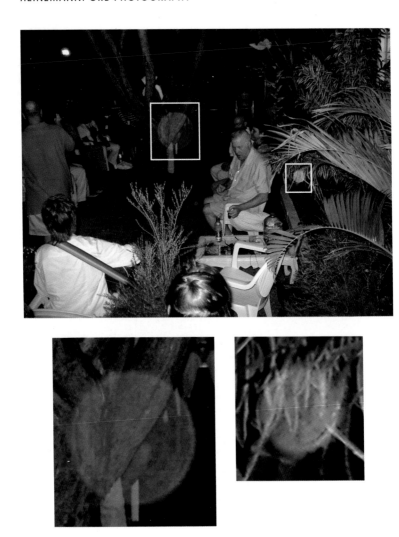

Figure II-19: Ron Roth teaching at a posada in Abadiânia, Brazil, at the occasion of a visit with John of God. (The white feature at the bottom of the large Spirit image is a portion of a bystander's leg positioned behind the tree; the Spirit being is in front of the tree.)

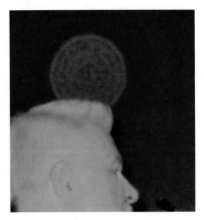

Figure II-20: Spirit-directed healing (Ron Roth intensive seminar in Scottsdale, Arizona, February 26, 2002). Note that the Spirit emanation is clearly positioned behind the Rev. Roth's head.

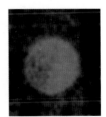

Figure II-21: Night scene in Abadiânia, Brazil, on May 23, 2005. The orb (further enlarged in the right figure) was identified by a clairvoyant consultant as an emanation from a certain highly evolved Spirit entity. It placed itself in a bush and is partially covered by leaves. (The bright spot in the center of the photo is the rising moon.)

Figure II-22: Ron Roth is teaching to a large audience. A second spirit emanation is present near the live video image projection screen on the left. Below: enlargements of details outlined above.

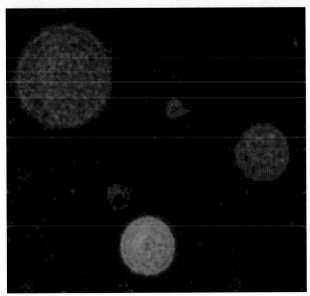

Figure II-23: Spirit (and nature spirit) emanations in the night sky above a posada in Abadiânia, Brazil, on May 20, 2005. I believe the smaller orbs in the image are nature spirits. Below: enlargement of the outlined area above.

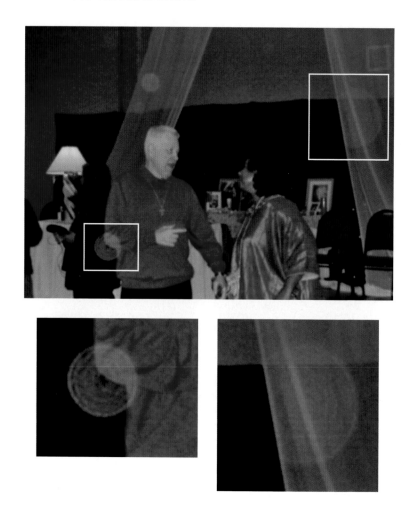

Figure II-24: Six Spirit emanations are present at a healing event with Ron Roth (February 2, 2003). The one at the healer's arm appears particularly purposefully positioned. The large one to the right unexpectedly does not protrude beyond the curtain into the black background.

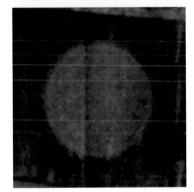

Figure II-25: At Sequoia Seminar, Ben Lomond, California, on June 11, 2005; two orbs showing their presence after my specific request to do so.

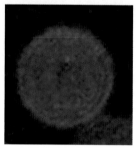

Figure II-26: "Fake" images of orbs, obtained by discharging a fine mist of water droplets close to the camera lens while taking the flash photograph. The interior (see magnified insert) is very similar to that of genuine orbs.

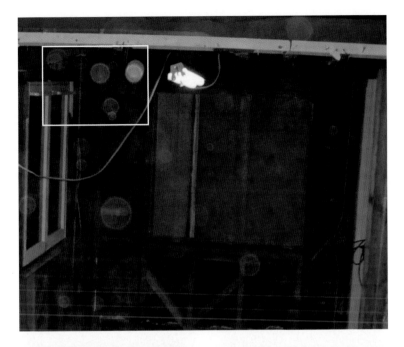

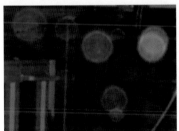 

Figure II-27: (Mostly) fake orbs; the photo was taken in a dusty room being prepared for remodeling. The outlined section was enlarged (lower left) and then color enhanced (lower right). The top right orb stands out as different in nature.

Figure II-28: Orb-like features in a photo taken in a dusty street in Chennai, India. The section containing the bicycle was enlarged (below) and slightly contrast enhanced. Hundreds of these low-intensity "fake orbs" literally "cloud" the image.

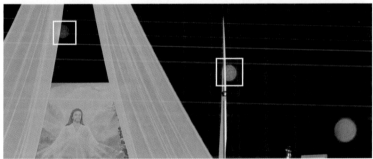

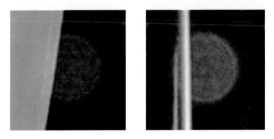

Figure II-29: At a prayer retreat with Ron Roth on November 11, 2005. Two orbs are partially eclipsed by objects between them and the camera lens. (Successive enlargements.)

Figure II-30: Monks at prayer, February 26, 2002; not electronically enhanced. There is movement in the bright image of a Spirit emanation in the top left of the photograph, which further attests to authenticity as photographed Spirit emanation.

Figure II-31: At a prayer retreat with Ron Roth on November 11, 2005, taken within one minute and not electronically enhanced. In both pictures, the brightness alone attests to authenticity as photographed Spirit emanations.

Figure II-32: Top: stereo image pair taken with two digital cameras with one flash, demonstrating that the person is seated well behind the plants and that the left plant is closer in the foreground than the right plant. Bottom: Enlargements of respective image sections, showing Spirit emanations of unequal size and locations.

Figure II-33: Stereo picture taken with two digital cameras and one (fully synchronized) flash in a dark hotel room. Three orbs are visible in the left photo.

(Photo by Art Runningbear; used with permission)

Figure II-34: This picture (not digitally enhanced!) came about after the person shown concentrated a strong field of thought next to his head and then announced that a photograph should be taken.

(a)

(b)

Figure II-35: Slightly different section of the two photographs in figure II-1, following identical color enhancement. Note the energetic field, showing up as green dots, around the person's torso and head, the triangle, and the Spirit being at the triangle in *a*, but not around the bright orb in *b*.

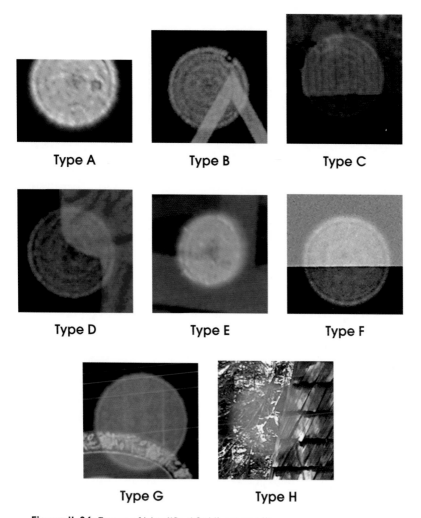

Figure II-36: Types of identified Spirit emanations:
Type A: Extremely bright, strong interior structure, unchanged by color enhancement; *Type B:* Lower intensity; rounded "eye"; *Type C:* Linear features; *Type D:* "Eye" in center; *Type E:* High intensity, fewer interior features, irregular bright spots; *Type F:* Low brightness, no "eye," mandala-like interior pattern; *Type G:* Low brightness and high-contrast periphery but virtually no interior pattern; *Type H:* High brightness, low contrast outer border, no interior pattern.

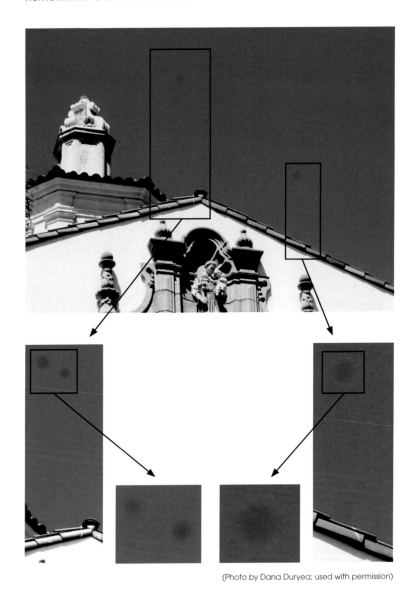

(Photo by Dana Duryea; used with permission)

Figure II-37: Images of dark spirits hovering above a historical building in Santa Barbara, California (contrast-enhanced).

that we can see *stereographically*, facilitated by our two eyes that are spatially apart from each other.

This stereo-visual principle can be used in photography if two cameras are mounted next to each other and precisely directed at the same scenery. Each camera takes a picture, and the two pictures, if taken at the same time, are essentially identical, except that one is taken from a slightly different angle than the other. They are stereo-pictures. If you look at both pictures in such a way that the left eye sees the left picture and the right eye sees the right picture and over-lap the two pictures into one, you get essentially the same stereo effect as you would by looking directly at the scene with both eyes. Usually, a device called a stereo viewer is used to facilitate the over-lapping of both pictures.

Some people are able to "strain" their eyes in such a way that they can get by without a stereo viewer. See the example in figure II-32, which shows photographs taken at a spiritual retreat with Ron Roth in early April 2006. If you get close to the picture, well within normal reading distance, and strain your eyes just a bit so you overlap both pictures in the center into one (disregarding the single picture you will still notice at either side), you will notice that the person is seated quite some distance behind the two plants.

It should be possible, then, to make stereo images of orbs with the same method. We have already established that the most important requirement for imaging orbs is that a flash is used. We have also already established that they move extremely fast. It will, therefore, be essential that the two pictures are taken *exactly* at the same time.

To achieve this, I set up an experiment in which the exposures of both cameras were taken with one and the same flash. To use camera A's flash, camera B's flash had to be inactivated and its shutter had to be open precisely at the time when the flash of camera A was at its peak. Then and only then would both pictures be exposed with the help of *one* flash and have their exposure moments be identical. This requires exact shutter synchronization of both cameras, which is not easy to achieve.

In order to circumvent the synchronization difficulties, I set camera B to a relatively long exposure time and manually released both shutters in such a way that, by trial and error, the synchronization happened to be achieved. After some testing, I was able to do this with a 1/4th of a second exposure time setting on camera B, achieving a "success rate" of better than 50 percent, meaning that in more than half of all stereo picture attempts thus taken, the exposures were indeed flash-synchronized.

In such experimental conditions, though, the room in which the photographs are taken must be relatively dark, so that camera B does not overexpose its image due to the long exposure time and the orbs, if there are any, still appear with enough contrast in both cameras.

In the top two pictures of figure II-32, synchronization was positive. The right picture is the one taken with camera A and with its built-in flash.[9] The left picture was taken with Camera B at 1/4th of a second exposure time and suppressed flash.[10] The overall colors in the

9. Camera A was a Nikon Coolpix 8800 camera with 8 megapixels resolution, using the built-in flash, in the regular flash photography mode.

10. Camera B was a 3.3-megapixel Pentax Optio 330 camera.

picture clearly reveal that the low color temperatures of the incandescent light in the room had a major impact on the image and that the requirement of a fairly dark room was only marginally met.

Nevertheless, the stereo pictures obtained in this experiment revealed interesting results: both pictures showed orbs, but they were not in the same position, nor of the same size! The result is demonstrated in the lower two pictures in figure II-32, which show magnifications of the respective top pictures. Specifically, the left image shows one small orb that is directly above the branch of the plant, whereas the right image shows two orbs that are to the right and left of that branch—clearly not the same orbs.

Why did we not see the same orbs in the two parts of the stereo picture? After all, we had the condition fulfilled that both parts were taken with the very same flash, and other conditions were met to the extent that orbs did show up in each of the two picture parts!

In order to further investigate this unexpected result, which was reproduced numerous times in stereo pictures taken at that retreat, we took additional stereo pictures, this time with two further constraints:

- They were taken in a strongly darkened room, so that camera B would not record anything if there was no flash synchronization.
- We held a strong intention to invite Spirit beings to exhibit their emanations and cooperate with the experiment.

The result is shown in figure II-33. This time, three orbs were clearly visible in the left part of the stereo picture, but none were visible in the right part! This time the cameras and the flash that produced the orb images were reversed. In figure II-32 it was the high-resolution Nikon camera with which the orbs were imaged, and in figure II-33 it was the lower-resolution Pentax camera, which further underlines that we are not "chasing" a camera effect.

What is *really* going on? More experimentation and observation led to some intriguing clues and helped us understand this effect. Before I elaborate on those, it is necessary to explain some of the other findings that informed my conclusions. In the "Intentionality and Directionality" section of the next chapter, we'll again pick up the issue of stereo photography—this time with further clues.

Images of Subtle Energy Field Concentrations

Throughout my study of orbs I have photographed some Spirit emanations that are decidedly different from the majority which I have observed. They are different in that they respond positively to digital color enhancement and/or have greatly different shapes or interior structures. In fact, light phenomena of various shapes and characteristics have been seen and reported at numerous occasions by people all over the world, and it would be highly presumptuous to even begin to get into this general topic in this book section. However, two particular non-orb light phenomena have consistently been observed in, or in connection with, photographs containing genuine orbs, and they should be mentioned for that reason.

Figure II-35 shows color-enhanced images of the two pictures presented in figure II-1. Let us first turn our attention to the orbs.

Both pictures were subjected to the same color enhancement process. In the upper figure, the orb turned blue/green (in other words, it responded to color enhancement), but in the lower image it remained white. This may be an indication of a different identity or a different class of Spirit emanations photographed in these two images, or it may be indicative of an ability of the Spirit being to change its appearance in a photograph as it wishes. While neither of these suggestions is scientific, the latter appears even less scientific than the former; but then, we must concede that we are dealing with phenomena that are outside of the realm of "normal" natural occurrences.

An interesting phenomenon can be observed around the torso of the person and around the triangle, as well as at the periphery of the image of the Spirit being in the upper photograph. It appears as if a spectrum of energy is being emitted that decays as the distance from the person or object increases. Also note that there is a color shift from more to less energetic features (blue to green in this case) as the distance increases. These two observations are characteristic of energy fields similar to those reported by people who can see auras. Again, since such fields are likely not emitting light in the visible spectrum—or else everybody would see them—we may assume that the nature of these fields is such that light from a flash is used to induce in them energetic quantum state changes with associated emission of photons in the visible light spectrum. The only difference would be that, in this case, some portions of the emitted light spectrum are missing, which would cause the color sensitivity.

Figure II-34 shows a picture of a light phenomenon that, at first glance, very much resembles a genuine orb, in that it is round, has

approximately the size of what we have become accustomed to identifying as an orb, and has the brightness of an orb. However, upon
closer examination you can see that the interior of this feature is substantially different from any of the other orbs discussed so far. There
are strong, asymmetric intensity distributions inside this orb-like
blotch. A similar phenomenon is shown in figure II-30 near the head
of the right person in the photograph. It should be noted that the
same photographs (not shown in figure II-34) also contain a "conventional" orb at a different location.

How did this picture come about? The person in the photograph is intuitive, clairvoyant, and fully aware that he is able to
produce a subtle energy field concentration outside his body on
command. As a matter of substantiation of this statement, he concentrated an intense field of thought energy by the side of his head
and, when he felt he had succeeded, requested that a picture be
taken. The result is figure II-34.

This evidence of a human projecting tangible energy to a position outside the body could help explain the underlying physics of
the space conditioning experiments and research on intention
imprinted electrical devices (IIEDs) by W. A. Tiller and colleagues.[11]
Their experiments clearly prove a measurable influence of a person's

11. One of Professor Tiller's famous experiments proving the effect of human intent on the outcome of simple physics experiments dates back to 1990 (see the bibliography). He tested whether
humans could influence the pulse counting rate of a gas discharge device by placing their hands close
to but not touching the device. If they *intended* to increase the pulse counting rate, an increase would
indeed occur. As soon as the participants were distracted, such as by focusing on simple mathematical
problems, the counts would decrease back to zero. These experiments were performed with many different test persons and under a variety of situations, and the basic result that human intent influences
the outcome was demonstrated beyond any reproach.

intent on the IIED. This influence must, by reasoning, be of a physical, energetic nature, because the changes they observed can only be explained on the basis of an *energetic* influence on the experiment.

The conditions leading to the orbs shown in figures II-30 and II-34 further indicate that this reasoning is correct. They are *energetic* features, or else they could not be recorded with a camera, and they are the consequence of the *intent* of the human subject. If a human is capable of projecting an energetic intent into a certain point close to his head, it must be assumed that he can also project energy into any other point in space of his choosing.[12]

Classifying Interior Features

In many cases, photographic enlargements of the orbs reveal an interior structure that appears to be unique to the particular Spirit. Even though several clairvoyant people have identified by name individual Spirits presented in these images, I'll refrain from going into that level of detail. I have two reasons: First, I personally do not have the degree of psychic ability that these individuals have—albeit I know them well and esteem them highly—and I do not wish to rely on hearsay in a matter of such importance, even though I have a high degree of confidence in them. Second, and more important, given that we are seeing *emanations* from Spirit beings, rather than the *entirety* of these beings, these emanations may well have certain "vibrational" aspects of the beings they originate from—and that is what clairvoyant people may

---

12. Numerous reports of distant healing can thus, in principle, be explained on the basis of a projection of intent.

be picking up. They will less likely have *optical, visual* features by which they can be identified.

However, it has become evident to me from this study that the orbs' interior features point to the presence of several *types* of Spirit emanations in the images. Whether these types represent classes or categories or hierarchical levels of Spirits is beyond my attempt of speculation.

I do find it noteworthy that on certain occasions, or in conjunction with certain individuals, the same *types* of Spirit emanations tend to appear. The Spirits who appeared at the September 26, 2004, event at two different locations (above the triangle and in it, figures II-1 and II-3) were likely different entities, as they show substantially different features. I have labeled them "Type A" and "Type B."

As mentioned earlier, Spirit Type A, seen in figure II-1b, stands out among all Spirit images I have ever photographed as *extremely* bright and essentially invariant to color and/or contrast level enhancement. It is not a simple flash of light. There is interior structure to the image—a structure clearly identified by the two aforementioned clairvoyant persons as a certain very high-level Spirit being. The physical evidence indicates that the image of this Spirit being likely consists of a *complete* color spectrum of wavelengths in the visible range; no one color is more emphasized than another—there is perfect *spectral harmony*.

The Type B Spirit image, observed in the triangle of figure II-3, is lower in intensity, albeit still clearly visible without electronic enhancement. It has an interior that appears similar to that of Type A, yet the features are softer, and the darker segment that appears like an "eye" is rounded, unlike the rectangular "eye" of Type A. I have observed Type

B Spirit emanation images at a number of occasions. For example, it was present at the consecration celebration in figure II-4.

A number of Spirit emanations were photographed at various occasions when Ron Roth performed healing/prayer services that are *similar* to Type B in appearance yet different enough to justify giving them a separate type classification. Type C was observed on January 30, 2004, when Ron Roth performed a healing in Abadiânia, Brazil. While the "eye" feature is similar to that observed in Type B, the interior shows some symmetric linear features that were not observed in other images. Note that there is a second being superimposed in the top left corner of this Type C being; it could not be identified.

Type D has relatively high-contrast concentric shapes, and the "eye" appears to be closer to the center. It does not exhibit strong symmetric features. It was frequently observed near or on Ron Roth, particularly when he performed healings. A typical example is shown in figure II-24.

The Spirit emanations photographed in figure II-11 also show an "eye" near the center, but the features of the rest of the interiority are substantially different from Types A through D. The interior features are less clearly defined and include randomly distributed small bright spots. I have named it Type E and included it in the summarizing figure of Spirit image types, figure II-36. Remarkable for Type E Spirits is that their images have relatively high intensity, clearly higher than Types B through D, which might possibly identify them as more highly evolved Spirits.

Yet another type of Spirit beings was found in photographs of events that did not have the connotation of being of a particularly "spiritual" nature, such as was shown in figures II-7 to II-10. These beings, identified as Types F and G in figure II-36, typically come through at somewhat lower intensity, have quite uniform, nondistinctive interiors, and do not appear to have an "eye." Type F has a nice, symmetric mandala-like interior pattern. It was present at the children's theater performance (figure II-8) in several of the few pictures I took. Type G appeared in a number of photos I took at a happy evening party during a Ron Roth seminar (figure II-7). It shows high contrast at the periphery but virtually no distinctive interior features, even though the imaging conditions were such that features should have been recorded if there were any. Without prejudice, and certainly without irrefutable facts to go by, I interpret the absence of distinct interior features as indicative of a specific, perhaps a somewhat less highly evolved, type of Spirit being.

In a few instances, I recorded orbs that had a poorly defined outer border. An example is shown in the brighter one of the two Spirit being images of figure II-25. It is possible that such an "effect" can occur when a Spirit being is photographed while it is in process of changing its size. This would explain why this fairly high-intensity image, which would indicate an evolved nature of the Spirit being photographed, has no interior features; they are simply blurred due to concentric motion. However, I cannot be certain about this interpretation and have, therefore, included it as "Type H" in figure II-36. It should be noted that the other being that showed up in figure II-25, "on command" as I explained in that paragraph, does have clear interior features that would resemble Type C.

Understanding
the Findings

Years of photographing Spirit emanations have given me many questions to ponder: What is it that we are seeing? How does it compare with what has been experienced by spiritual visionaries, such as those who received the apparitions of the Holy Mother at Medjugorje? Why at this time?

In this chapter, I attempt to answer some of these questions and offer some understanding of my findings. I'll also discuss what I have learned from photographing dark spirits.

Comparison with the Apparitions at Medjugorje

In the early 1980s (mostly in 1981 to 1984), apparitions of the Holy Mother in the then-Yugoslav village of Medjugorje received world-wide attention. Approximately forty children and young adults between the ages of ten and twenty saw these apparitions during a span of several years, typically occurring once a day for an average duration of about one minute. More than one thousand apparitions were counted through 1984.

These apparitions "allegedly" occurred to the visionaries in the form of "real" appearances of the Holy Mother and "real" sensory engagement in a form quite similar to *conversations*, as opposed to *images* that may have been imprinted into their minds by another dimension.[1] The recipients of the apparitions asked questions and received answers; they credibly stated that they "saw" and "heard" the Holy Mother. But while brain wave measurements confirmed brain activity expected and normal during conversations, it was scientifically established that the physical auditory and visual sensory organs of the visionaries were not involved. Other people around them, including the scientists who did extensive testing on the children during many of the apparitions, did not hear or see *anything* that was going on.

The experiences of these children were considered so extraordinary that a number of studies were made to substantiate their authenticity and rule out that they were hallucinations or willful misstatements. Arguably the most compelling scientific report on these studies was published in 1985 by René Laurentin and Henri Joyeux (see the bibliography). The various scientific studies included electrocardiograms, brain wave measurements, audio tests, visual

---

1. I am using the word *allegedly* because there is no actual scientific *proof* of the authenticity of these apparitions. However, I use quotation marks to signify that, after having studied the extensive research performed and published on the subject, I feel that the conclusion of authenticity is compelling.

tests, blood pressure tests, and extensive psychological tests on the visionaries who saw the apparitions.

A major conclusion from these studies is that the apparitions are being perceived as contacts with a representative of the *eternal reality*.[2] The authors conclude that certain individuals received the grace to be the objects for these contacts and that the actual form of the contacts bypassed the visual/auditory/sensory faculties of the recipients and went directly to their minds. All this was unequivocally concluded from the scientific test results. The psychological tests confirmed that the subjects were healthy, represented a wide spectrum of character and mentality, and that hallucination or any sort of foul play could be ruled out.

They believe that the apparitions originated with the subject (in this case, the Divine Mother) from the *eternal reality*. They suggest that the means, or the available methods, of the eternal reality are immensely greater than the means of the physical reality and that it is, therefore, "easily" possible for beings from within the eternal reality to devise a mechanism of communication with humans that extends into the very core of human perception.[3]

Looking Beyond Medjugorje

Laurentin and Joyeux also hypothesize that the apparitions must have had a specific purpose that likely went well beyond the mere intent

2. The use of this term *eternal reality* by Laurentin and Joyeux is entirely congruent with what others and I have called the *Spiritual* or *divine* reality.

3. This conclusion is entirely congruent with my own conclusion about this subject matter, which I presented in my books *Consciousness or Entropy?* and *Expanding Perception*.

to establish direct contact with these individuals. However, they did not elaborate on that notion. We now hypothesize that the purpose may have been to establish credibility among the critical, disbelieving human race at large. In spite of the overwhelming evidence— albeit all anecdotal in the critics' eyes—that the Spiritual realm is for real, a domineering fraction of humanity acts as if it were not, and this misguided action has brought the world to the brink of self-destruction. Acceptance of the Spiritual reality will receive a strong boost, perhaps the boost that will bring humanity over the hump, when it becomes credible in the eyes of the scientific community.[4]

If this was indeed the primary intent of the apparitions, it is unfortunate that it was not—or was only marginally—successful. The magnificent events of Medjugorje were never publicized to the extent that they became known and accepted *by the public at large.* They rather remained an "interesting spiritual phenomenon," of which only a relatively small number of people became aware over the years. Furthermore, the influence of the skeptics remained so strong that, in spite of the compelling reports written about the apparitions, the overall—deplorably now turned historic—view of these events is that they are to be brushed away as hallucinations or some other aberration. And now, some twenty years later, even a copy of the excellent book by Laurentin and Joyeux has become almost impossible to come by.

---

4. A boost will undoubtedly also come through a variety of other mechanisms, including world-wide "awakening" movements, such as the "Oneness Movement" that originated about a decade ago in Southern India (with Sri Bhagwan and Sri Amma) and is now rapidly gaining momentum on all continents. But these spiritual movements will likely not, or only very sluggishly, reach the scientifically oriented communities. So both approaches are clearly needed.

Many people, and probably most of those reading this book, include in their belief system the notion that a Spiritual reality exists and that our physical reality is some sort of extension from it. They view their lives as being in the context of that larger reality, and this view gives them a sense of purpose.

I hypothesize that highly evolved Spirit beings in the Spiritual reality see that humanity is in dire need of discovering its purpose and that they devised phenomenal occurrences, such as the apparitions of Medjugorje, to help mankind in this epochal jump in consciousness. Medjugorje could have been it, but, collectively, we were too dumb— or more likely too enamored with our misguided understanding of "science"—to accept it. There was not enough "realism" in it. The apparitions were a *primary* experience to just a very small number of people. To all others, they were of *secondary* nature, no more than hearsay. There was no ironclad scientific proof, no picture, nothing that could be introduced into the *Annals of Physics* as scientific evidence.

In this regard, a significant observation at the last apparition reported to have occurred in Medjugorje should be mentioned. All five of the visionaries who saw the apparition independently stated to the scientists testing them that the last words of the Virgin Mother were that "there will be no more apparitions of the Holy Mother on this Earth" (Laurentin and Joyeux). None of the visionaries expanded on this statement despite the bombardment of questions thrown back at them. They all stated that this was "all the Virgin Mother said" and they were sorry that they did not ask her for more clarification.

Perhaps, so the hypothesis continues, we can look at the emer- gence of photography of Spirit emanations as another attempt from the Spirit world, likely one among many, in that direction. This time, the "apparitions" go a step further. This time they deliver *irrefutable scientific evidence* in the form of photos. Photos are not just visible to a handful of people while the rest of us are excluded in the *direct* perception of what is going on. Photos are visible to *everybody*—this time, the *evidence* is available to everybody. There are no longer prerequisites, such as having extraordinary psychic abilities. The evidence is indiscriminately available to anyone who makes the effort to look at it.

If my hypothesis of the Spirits' intent is correct, this time around "they" have a better chance of succeeding. This is because it is actually the *duty* of scientists to look at physical evidence that presents itself. To look the other way is not really fitting for a good scientist. This time, the evidence is directly pointed at the scientific community.

Pictures as Emanations from Another Dimension

In chapter 8, I discussed a simple metaphor to describe the nature of an emanation. I explained that a genuine orb is likely an emanation from a Spirit being, i.e., something *flowing from the essence* of a Spirit being; but it is, of course, not an image of the *entirety* of the Spirit being itself. It is not even like a photo of a person, which only reflects the person's physical characteristics and does not give any credible clues regarding the person's mental, emotional, or spiritual qualities. Instead, it is very likely that a genuine orb is even less to a Spirit being than a photograph of a person is to the person photographed.

What then does the orb represent from the essence of a Spirit being that makes it significant? We must consider two important features:

- First and foremost, an orb is a *physical* manifestation. As discussed earlier, we must assume that the Spirit being has a mechanism to manifest itself in such a way that it can be detected with physical means. In this particular case, the manifestation is such that it can be detected as light, i.e., as electromagnetic waves in the visible spectral range.
- Second, the orb's mobility must be assumed to be entirely *directed and controlled* by the Spirit being from which it emanates—just as an automobile's headlights are directed and controlled by the human driver.

These two points warrant more discussion. Humankind's experience with apparitions (the most powerful and most scientifically credible ones ever reported appear to be the earlier discussed apparitions of the Holy Mother at Medjugorje) indicate that in certain circumstances Spirits do have the capability of manifesting themselves *physically*, even though this has been extremely rare.[5] If we discard some, or even the majority, of the apparitions that have been reported over time, due to—in the critics' view—lack of scientific studies that distinguish them from hallucinations or other disqualifying constructs, I consider the research done on the apparitions at Medjugorje alone as sufficient evidence for this point.

The second point is the more important of the two and, at the same time, the more obvious and plausible. *If* the orb is an emanation

---

5. The apparitions at Medjugorje were actually not of a physical nature, but the people receiving them (the "visionaries") were clearly perceiving them and processing them with their physical faculties (their minds).

from a Spirit being, it does not take much of a stretch in imagination to think that the Spirit being from which it emanates entirely controls its mobility, size, appearance, and so on. It is then irrelevant for the conclusions we draw in this section if the orb is a picture of a Spirit being *itself* or just of an *emanation from it*. Both would lead to the same conclusions that Spirit beings are

- all around us
- highly evolved and intelligent
- capable of changing their size and location extremely quickly

We can summarize these conclusions in one important statement: *Photographs of Spirit emanations offer evidence—as close to scientific proof as we have ever come in proving the existence of the Spiritual reality—that Divine Presence is real.* I must add a disclaimer to this statement: It is intended for the critic, the nonbeliever, rather than to spiritually aware people to whom the Spiritual reality is nothing less than a "real" reality. I direct the statement at the person who comes from the conventional viewpoint where *scientific proof* is the *only* acceptable evidence. If one adopts such a standard, then essentially everything our clerics in the churches, synagogues, and mosques as well as our spiritually inclined fellow human beings have ever reported is nothing but anecdotal evidence. Not much, if anything, remains that meets the standard of *proof* of Spiritual reality's existence.

I maintain that the immense totality of such spiritual evidence—albeit each *individual* evidence being anecdotal—should add up to being more than sufficient proof, even for the "fundamentalist" scientist.

Frequency of Appearance and Other Factors

As I mentioned in reference to figure II-16, a large number of orbs in a photograph might suggest a certain quality—"the more, the better." I'd like to discuss this in more detail.

It would certainly be a "human" logic and characteristic to draw such a conclusion. However, this human logic may not necessarily hold when it comes to the Spiritual reality. The number of Spirit emanation images appearing in a photograph should not be taken as indicative of anything other than that these Spirits *chose to make their presence known/seen* in the particular photo. There can only be speculation as to the reasons or to the identities of the Spirits involved. No event is "good" or "not good" or "superior" or "inferior" judged solely on how many orbs can be distinguished in photos taken. Nor should the position of such orbs, the photographer, or people in the photo be the subject of such specific conclusion. We should simply assume that *the Spirits have chosen to be visible in a particular photo and, perhaps, in a particular position, for whatever reason they might have.*

Having said this, I wish to make a few comments. The number of pictures I have taken that contain genuine Spirit emanations has skyrocketed since September 2004, when I started seeing them, probably by a factor of 100, as I already mentioned. Furthermore, other people are seeing them more and more frequently as well. I have received numerous pictures with orbs from people who know about my interest in this subject. Even though many of them appear to be diffraction/reflection effects from dust particles or moisture droplets, a good number are genuine, and that number also seems to be rising quickly.

On the basis of these facts, my earlier explanation is hard to reject: The Spirit world may have a specific intent associated with these sightings, and this intent may be that they want people to know that the world of the Spirit is for real and, perhaps, that there is great concern in that realm about the course on which humanity is heading.[6]

Although I realize that I am going out on a limb, I also suspect that the Spirit emanations' various positions in photographs may be suggesting the same thing. For example, the position under the prayer basket (figure II-12) appears to be more than coincidental. The positioning at the healer's head (figure II-20) or arm (figure II-24) appears to pronounce, "Listen to the spiritual teachers!" and "Be healed!" The circumstance that orbs often appear at genuinely joyous events (figure II-7) seems to underline that the Spirit world desires joy for humanity. And the tendency of showing up around children (figures II-5, II-8, II-9, and II-10) seems to tell us that they care for those who will "inherit this earth." There appears to be an irrefutable connection with *intentionality*!

Intentionality and Directionality

I promised we would return to the subject of stereo pictures that we left in the previous chapter. What else was happening when figure II-33 was taken? What is it that might have caused the orbs to show up only in one but not the other half of the stereo image pair?

6. The second part of this assumption is my own interpretation. It is based on the observation that spiritually conscious people's political, sociological, and environmental concerns are congruent with the realization that humanity's present course will eventually lead to global disaster.

In preparation for taking those pictures, I had invited a good friend with remarkable subtle energy perception to visit me and my wife in our hotel room for an "experiment." I asked him to collaborate in asking certain Spirit beings to reveal themselves in a specific attempt to produce a stereo image of their emanation. He consented to the experiment, and the stereo image shown in figure II-33 resulted.

When our friend saw the pictures, he immediately identified one of the two smaller orbs as one of his Spirit Guides whom he had requested to show up in the experiment. He simply identified that one, because he "felt it being at that location when the picture was taken." He also stated that he had received a communication from this Spirit Guide that "most likely the experiment would not yield the result I had expected" and that "the Spirit [emanations] would only be visible in *one* camera, not in both."

Why would this be? Why did it indeed *not* show up in both cameras? After all, the experiment was flawless. One and the same flash, with a duration of just about 1/1000th of a second, caused the image recording in *both* cameras. The orb imaged with one of the cameras was without a shadow of a doubt genuine. Yet the other camera did not record an orb in the same location!

This astonishing result may have to do with *directionality*. The fact that a light emanating from a source located a few feet away from two cameras that are positioned a few inches apart from each other would reach *only one* but not the other camera can be explained only if the light were *highly directional*, similar to a laser beam.

If this were indeed the correct conclusion, it would explain a number of noteworthy observations:

- Highly directional light is likely *coherent;* in other words, its undisturbed wave front is unidirectional, and the photons are *in phase* with each other. When coherent light transmits through a strong energetic field, such as we can assume is happening in the energetic globe from which it originates, characteristic phase shifts are expected to occur in the emitted light beams that can cause interference phenomena in an image plane orthogonal to the direction in which the light is traveling—such as in our digital camera.[7] These interference phenomena can explain the concentric, Fresnel fringe–like intensity distributions often observed in orb images.

- These concentric intensity distributions would be expected to look similar to out-of-focus images, such as we have in the case of "fake orbs." We would thus have a plausible explanation for why fake and real orbs look so much alike.

- Given the directionality of these emanating light beams, it would essentially be impossible to argue that images of Spirit emanations are random events. If they were random, the likelihood of a laser-like directional beam *precisely* aiming at a camera lens at a distance of several dozen feet, and doing this in the extremely short moment that the camera shutter happens to be open, would be very low indeed; actually observing an orb based on such low coincidental probabilities would be *extremely* unlikely. As it is, the directionality would have to be assumed to be *intentional*. In other words, the Spirit beings

7. See " The Photographic Process" in chapter 9.

must be *wanting* to direct their light beams into the camera—
they must be *wanting to be seen*.[8]

- To direct a strongly directional, coherent light beam succes-
sively into *two* camera lenses within the short duration of one
flash, with equal light quantity going into each camera, so
that it could be detected with both cameras—as I had envi-
sioned the outcome to be—might well be a task too difficult
even for powerful Spirit beings, given the limited experimental physical conditions at hand.

I had, therefore, been expecting the impossible, and "they" did
the best they could under the circumstances, which is to show up in
one *or* the other camera (regardless of which one produced the flash)
but not *simultaneously* in both.

The conclusion that Spirit beings *want* to be seen with digital
cameras under certain circumstances they select at will is congruent
with modern physics. We know now that we live in a *participatory* universe. The assumption that a physical experiment can be devised that
would have a *definite, certain* outcome is no longer valid. The observer,
the individual staging the experiment, becomes a *participant* in the
experiment, and his participation affects the outcome.

In photography of true orbs, the photographer, through his
intention, has *some* influence with regard to the appearance of orbs in

---

8. A critic might argue that the flash might induce secondary light emission that is directed to it
(the flash) rather than being isotropic. The experiments disprove this argument, because orbs were
seen and not seen randomly with either camera, the one that provided the flash and the one that just
had the shutter open but did not produce a flash.

his pictures. It is not just a matter of pure chance whether or not orbs show up in your photos; you yourself have some influence on it. It is not clear what this influence might be, and it is certainly not a question of you being "better" than anyone else in any respect— with the exception, perhaps, that your state of openness toward the occurrence of such image features may play a role in the Spirit's selection of your camera, rather than someone else's, to record its emanation.

Dark Energies: Low-evolved Spirits

So far in this book I have focused on emanations of highly evolved Spirit beings. However, it may be the case that not all Spirits are equally highly evolved but that, instead, a huge spectrum of consciousness exists in the Spiritual reality. This may range anywhere from that of "archangels" to entities so poorly evolved that they are unaware that they no longer exist in the physical realm and cling to perennial earthbound existence (until they are eventually assisted in their journey to the higher levels of spiritual beings). In this section, we will take a very cursory look at photographic evidence of lower evolved spirit beings. We will do so to the extent that it relates to, and compares to, photographing emanations of highly evolved Spirit beings.

As I mentioned in the introduction, a friend gave me a series of photos exhibiting what was interpreted to be "dark spirits." One of them is shown in figure II-37. My friend and his crew had been hired to clear a well-known historical building in Southern California from what was believed to be earthbound spirit beings. The photo shows three dark areas that were distinguishable at different locations in subsequent photos, and they assumed them to be orbs from low-evolved spirits.

The following observations show how these orbs were different from the orbs I have so far presented:

- The orb-like features were distinctly *darker* than their surroundings, unlike any other orbs I had previously noticed.
- The contrast of the features in the original photographs was very low.
- There was no reaction to color enhancement, and only very minor improvement in the features' visibility could be achieved with electronic contrast enhancement.
- There is some evidence of a higher-intensity ring around the dark area, similar to an optical Fresnel (diffraction) ring (see the lower right of figure II-37).
- None of the photos I had previously taken—albeit all in settings that were presumably congenial for the presence of *highly* evolved Spirits—showed any such features.

These findings corroborate with our overall discussion of how highly evolved Spirits select to be seen and what the mechanism of their visibility might be. In this case of imaging low-evolved spirits, rather than emitting visible light into the digital camera in which they *want* to be recorded, as would be the case for enlightened Spirits, dark spirits would deliberately *not* want to be seen, or would not have the intelligence and means at their avail to be seen. The physics behind seeing dark round spots in a digital camera would suggest that these dark spirits do have a localized, concentrated, concentric energy field that is capable of absorbing and/or diffracting visible light and, therefore, *removing* (rather than adding to) illumination picked up by the camera—hence the dark spots. Our observation of a diffraction fringe around the dark area strengthens this explanation.[9]

It is noteworthy that we did not find *any* evidence of such dark orbs in any of several hundred pictures that *do* show emanations of evolved ("light") Spirits, nor in thousands of pictures taken at the same general occasions but not showing any orbs.[10] Even though many of these pictures have a dark backdrop that would make it inherently difficult to see dark features, even with state-of-the-art contrast enhancement techniques, there are enough pictures that do exhibit lighter colored room walls and ceilings that would be expected to allow for seeing such contrast changes if they were present. One can therefore conclude that dark beings do not feel welcome anywhere in the vicinity of light beings and simply are not—or only in extremely rare situations—present.

Furthermore, the imaging mode of absorption/diffraction rather than emission does not allow for the extreme directionality that we have seen in the case of emanations from evolved Spirits, since the

---

9. It also strengthens a conclusion that the energy field of dark spirits is not actually strong enough to *absorb* physical light but, instead, simply slightly *deflects* it.

10. As we have concluded in the preceding chapter, not seeing emanations of evolved Spirit beings in a digital photograph does not indicate that they are not present.

light that is absorbed or diffracted at dark spirits is usually non-directional. One would, therefore, expect to see dark beings of this kind in photographs with any camera, taken by any photographer, and without conscious influence of the dark being or the photographer. The occurrence of photographs showing a dark being—albeit generally with a very low degree of contrast—should, therefore, *relatively* be much more frequent than is the case for photographing intelligent light beings. Since they have, in fact, been observed only rarely, we can conclude that only *relatively* very few such dark beings exist. The "cloud of witnesses around us" seems to consist of light beings.

• • •

The late British astrophysicist Sir Fred Hoyle predicted in the 1950s that after we were able to take a photograph of the earth from outer space, humanity would experience a profound leap in consciousness. This prediction was elegantly confirmed in recent kinesiology studies by psychiatrist Dr. David R. Hawkins. Might there perhaps be the suggestion of a similar supposition that the advent of photography of orbs by anybody who has a digital camera marks the beginning of yet another quantum-step rise in human consciousness?

This time, it would be that we begin to see ourselves not only as participants of a *physical* experience but also as members of a higher-order reality that is beyond the classical physical realm. This realm—I call it the Spiritual reality—and our physical reality are one. You and I, as members of both, are one with both.

Orb pictures undeniably remind us that there is more to life than what the traditional human "realist" would have conceded. It is my hope that they will convince more and more realists that the reality in which they have seen themselves is far, far too limiting to be concidered all there is. The invisible cloud of witnesses around us has become visible, and its message is unfolding.

Afterword

Spirit Emanations and Spirit-directed Healing

Throughout these chapters I have shown many photographs that I have taken at spiritual healing events. I'd like to add a word about spirit-directed healing, since my work with orbs has naturally made me wonder how spirit-directed healing and orbs are related.

We understand that the art of curing physical ailments has been overwhelmingly demonstrated by numerous healers. Yet we do not know what *really* happens in a spiritual healing event— how spiritual *intent, wisdom, and direction* are transformed into physical energy that is applied to very specific locations in a patient's body for the physical healing to manifest.

My work with photographing Spirit emanations has led me to some conclusions regarding the mechanisms involved in spirit-directed healing. I'd like to present a hypothesis of how it might work, based on Spirit emanations' characteristics. As you will see, modern-day Spirit-directed healing agrees with this hypothesis.

What Is Spirit-directed Healing?

While this is a string of three very commonly used words, the term *Spirit-directed healing* has been coined only recently by the spiritual healer Ron Roth. In Spirit-directed healing, the healing action is not directed by the healer. The healer is simply a channel for the healing power to flow through to (i.e., "be directed to") the patient. The source of the healing energy is attributed to the infinite power intrinsic to the Spiritual reality, and the ultimate "director" of the healing activity is the Holy Spirit, or Holy Spirits.[1]

There are several mechanisms by which this seems to work. However, as we will find out, a distinction between these mechanisms may end up being arbitrary. Healings performed by Ron Roth frequently look like direct "blasts" of healing power. This would be in contrast to healing through mediumship, where the healer acts as a medium through whom Spirits work. This form of Spirit-directed healing is, for example, practiced by the Brazilian healer John of God. He acts as a medium between a highly evolved Spirit being and the patient. The Spirit being, any one of about thirty "entities" who work through John of God to perform "surgeries," appears to incorporate into his body and literally takes charge of what is occurring. The insights we have derived from studying photographs of Spirit emanations help in the understanding of how these evolved Spirits or entities might actually be performing their remedial work on a patient's physical body.

Surgeries at the Casa de Dom Inácio

In the Casa de Dom Inácio in Abadiânia, Brazil, John of God performs two kinds of Spirit-directed surgeries: visible and invisible. Invisible surgeries take place much more frequently than visible sur-

---

1. I use the plural form deliberately. It implies that there is a world of Spirits, with a hierarchical multitude of Spirit beings, rather than just one immensely powerful yet somewhat elusive, nondescript conglomerate of nonphysical energy and cosmic consciousness that a person with Judeo-Christian heritage often associates with the "Holy Spirit."

geries, and the helpers at the Casa insist that invisible surgeries are just as effective as the visible ones. They state that the main purpose of *visible* surgeries is to be able to demonstrate to the skeptics that something "real" is actually happening. Witnessing a visible surgery, without anesthesia and with steel "tools" that mysteriously *change their physical form when they are introduced into the body*, does a great deal toward expelling that skepticism, even for the strongest doubter.

A clairvoyant person has confided to me that she sees the auric field of the surgery patient, not the physical body, and she sees John of God working on the energetic body of the person rather than on the physical body. How does surgery on the nonphysical body of the patient manifest in the physical body? How does it happen that, as a consequence of visible or invisible surgery by the entities at the Casa, cancer cells are removed, tumors shrink and/or are encapsulated so they will remain in remission, diabetes is cured, bone fractures are rapidly healed, rashes removed, blindness cured, hearing loss restored, and the like? What is really happening here? Our results from the study of photography of Spirit emanations may cast some light on this mystery.

Critical Features of Spirit Emanations for Healing

From our study of photographing orbs we have concluded, among other findings:

Spirits have an extremely high mobility

In conjunction with figures II-2 and II-10, we determined that the Spirit photographed must have moved at a speed well over several hundred miles per hour. While this may seem high, there is reason to conjecture that this type of velocity is actually at the very low end of what is possible and usually happening in the Spiritual reality. *Usual, normal* speeds of mobility of Spirits may well be many orders of magnitude faster. The reason for relatively rarely seeing Spirit emanations in photographs may well *not* be that they are seldom present but that they are usually moving so fast that there is absolutely no way to capture them in a photograph—except if they *want* to be photographed and slow down.

Spirit emanations can rapidly expand and contract

In figures II-4 and II-9, presumably the same Spirit being expanded in size between the two exposures. Again, I believe that these are very extraordinary examples—extraordinary in the *slow* speed of expansion demonstrated in the pictures. The reason for only very rarely seeing the same Spirit being in two subsequent images may well be that they usually expand at such high velocity that this would make it impossible to capture them in subsequent photographs.[2]

It is thinkable that the Spirit being's *mechanism* of motion is actually based on expansion and contraction: expansion to such a size that the intended new location is now included within its sphere of presence, followed by contraction with that precise location remaining in the sphere of presence. This could be understood as

---

2. Also, since their "normal" mode of presence is being in motion, holding still for the duration of a photographic exposure may be "usually" as unrealistic as that of a four-year-old child sitting still through a church worship service.

occurring over vast distances, even intergalactic distances—there would be no limit.

However, the hypothesis of an explanation for Spirit-directed healing does not hinge on this assumption of a *mechanism* of mobility. What it does hinge on is the logical consequence of being able to expand and contract an *energetic sphere*: since the *total* energy of a Spirit emanation could be assumed to remain approximately constant during an expansion/contraction sequence, regardless of the size or volume it happens to occupy, its energy *density* changes greatly with expansion and contraction. The smaller the size, the higher is its energy density.

Thus, it is conceivable that Spirit emanations can contract to diameters that are so small that the energy *density* they attain in the small volume they are then taking up is comparatively very high. If the volume contracts to *extremely* small sizes, such as to that of cells or even molecules or atoms, the energy density they can then obtain is enormous, plausibly more than enough to profoundly affect states of physical objects—sufficient to break or induce chemical bonds, or even vaporize entire cells.

Spirits are highly intelligent

If the fact that we are able to photograph Spirit emanations at all were not enough evidence of their intelligence per se, our experience communicating with orbs (see figure II-25) or our conclusions from stereo photography of orbs (figures II-32 and II-33) offer that evidence.

It is, in fact, not unreasonable to assume that the intelligence of evolved Spirits greatly surpasses human intelligence. Many teachers and spiritual leaders have argued that consciousness is manifest in the Spiritual reality, where it moves at essentially infinite velocities and is not subject to decay but will remain available to tap into *at any point in time* by any being with a capability and will to do so.[3]

Evolved Spirits are assumed to have this ability. We might, perhaps, compare this with the potential we humans have by virtue of the Internet, with two very significant differences: Our access to the *information* on the Internet is limited in terms of access speed and data processing capabilities; and, furthermore, we can only find information on the Internet, not the other "products" of human consciousness, such as *feelings, compassion,* or *love.*[4] From our physical (human) frame of reference, Spirits will be able to acquire information and knowledge of all varieties *with essentially infinite speed*, and they will be able to *act upon that information infinitely fast.*

However, even in that circumstance of infinite *capability*, we must assume that Spirits will *not automatically* act and do, on our behalf, what they are capable of doing. We must assume that an action on their part has to be triggered by some sort of communication. They are immensely intelligent and can acquire a wealth of information in minute fractions of (physical) time, but they will likely not put that intelligence to use on our behalf *unless they are so motivated*.

3. This is also taught as an important principle at the Oneness University in the Golden City in Southern India. It is also a key teaching of the Abraham-Hicks material and of the Jacob-Gorman Groups.

4. This renders the comparison with the Internet quite weak, indeed, because the difference between what is available in the Spiritual reality and what can be found online is, and will remain, *immense*, in spite of all technological advancements.

The Hypothesis for Divine Healing

With these three characteristics of Spirit emanations—fast mobility, the ability to rapidly change size, and intelligence—we have the foundation to formulate a hypothesis of a mechanism for Spirit-directed healing:

- Through an emanation into the physical reality, an evolved Spirit being is able to become active within a person's body and can, by a series of contractions to a tiny high-energy density sphere and subsequent expansion, selectively correct a deficiency by breaking or reestablishing chemical bonds, or even vaporizing entire cells or cell blocks.

- Evolved Spirits possess, or can essentially instantly acquire, the intelligence and information required for applying this ability toward the task of curing physical ailments in people. This task is then understood as an extremely long string of single energetic interventions. However, since the speed with which this can occur is essentially unlimited, even billions of such cellular, molecular, or atomic-size "healing" events can occur within a fraction of a "moment."

- Consequently, one evolved Spirit entity alone is capable of performing many healing events on many people within a very short time.

- The healing ability is limitless. However, its occurrence is upon request only; it will not necessarily occur without "mobilization."

Let us apply the hypothesis to the situation of a person diagnosed with metastasized cancer. According to the first part of the hypothesis, a Spirit being would be capable of reducing the size of its energy field to the tiny size of tissue cells and converge that contracted/concentrated energy field precisely onto a spot where it is needed, such as on a cluster of cancer cells that need to be incapacitated. It could thus do precisely what would "conventionally" be achieved with radiation therapy or chemotherapy—with the added advantage of molecular-size precision. Depending on the amount of energy focused on the cell or onto a certain molecule within it, it could break an active bond that might be the cause for its pathological behavior, reestablish a bond that might have been broken and caused erroneous cell functioning, repair genetic pathology, do whatever is required to heal cells or DNA, or entirely "vaporize" pathological tissue or isolate it from doing further damage.

According to the second part of the hypothesis, the Spirit being would instantly acquire the knowledge of what precisely is wrong with the patient, which cells have what kind of pathological behavior, and how to take care of that problem. It would be able to do this in extremely rapid succession, cell by cell, regardless of the total number that needs to be addressed. Analysis, contraction into the precise location, expansion: this process repeated over and over, billions of times if needed, in a fraction of a second!

Not being subject to the physical limitations of speed, the size of the tumor is really not of primary concern. Once done with one patient, in a fraction of an instant, the healing Spirit would be able to concentrate its attention on the next person, and the next one, and the next.... The ultimate "limitation" would only be the desire, or readiness, of the patient to get that healing "work" done. Since the patient's thought processes occur in the same realm as where the Spirits operate (the Spiritual reality), the two can clash when the patient consciously or even unconsciously communicates disbelief in the Spirits' ability to heal.

"Invisible" Spiritual Surgeries

The evidence presented in this section does indeed point to this being a possible mechanism for Spiritual healing—certainly not the only one, but perhaps one of a variety of mechanisms. It appears that what is happening in Brazil lends credence to our hypothesis.

Let us look at the invisible surgeries being performed there. Twice each day when the Casa is open, at the beginning of the morning and afternoon sessions, invisible surgeries take place. In each case, they are administered "simultaneously" to one entire group of individuals. The recipients, as many as one hundred people, are seated as a group in a room. After a short introduction and a prayer, the surgery takes place while the recipients remain seated, typically with their eyes closed. Some people can sense that something is happening to their bodies, others feel little or nothing. Nobody really knows where in the body the surgery is taking place. After a few minutes, the end of the surgery session is announced, and people are ushered outside to a "recovery area." Here they are reminded that they just underwent surgery, regardless of what they may have sensed, and need a rest period.

Most people, even those who felt nothing, will soon experience that something indeed has happened inside their bodies and will gladly follow the suggested resting instructions.

Our hypothesis agrees with the entire sequence of events. The preselection process meets the requirement that the patient must be the initiator for the process. The group situation and the short time required for the surgeries on all people in the group are, as pointed out, possibly due to the high velocities available in the Spiritual reality. The finding that many patients do not even sense that a surgery has taken place follows from the circumstance that no incision is required for the surgery; no (or only a minimum number of) nerve cells are affected; and the surgery does not compromise unnecessary amounts of healthy tissue but is confined to the pathological cells, organs, or tissue. The need for recuperation is reasonable, because, after all, a surgery has taken place, and the circumstance that a large fraction of the people who have undergone invisible surgery will feel weak and sore after the surgery makes sense for the same reason.

It is said that certain spiritual entities who have worked in the medical field during their most recent incarnation are the primary Spirits performing surgery at the Casa. The fact that many entities do *not* have that "background" and are as effective as those who do attests that the actual *knowledge* required to perform these surgeries can be acquired by *any* evolved Spirit entity. It may, however, be true that in the Spirit world, just as in our physical world, Spirit entities do what they like to do and are inclined to do. This may explain why those that had medical "careers" in their human lifetimes may more likely want to lend their talent to the cause of spiritual healing than others who pursued different human endeavors in their incarnate state.

"Visible" Spiritual Surgeries

What about the *visible* surgeries at the Casa and the kind of healing practiced by spiritual healers like Ron Roth or, decades ago, Aimee Semple McPherson and Kathryn Kuhlman (see the bibliography)?

The latter may, in fact, be much less different from invisible surgeries, as we discussed them, than it appears at first glance. The energy "zapping" that many people experience when touched by a healer like Ron Roth may well be understood as nothing other than the healing action performed by a Spirit entity in accordance with the hypothesis. The sensation experienced by people in such circumstances, a certain weakness hours or even days following such an event, and the miraculous healings reported at large do fit the pattern described in the hypothesis.

The phenomenon of visible surgeries at the Casa de Dom Inácio and at various other locations, mostly in Brazil and the Philippines, is extremely interesting. As I mentioned earlier, the primary reason for visible surgeries is said to be for the benefit of the onlookers, or even the patient himself, who will be easier convinced of the healing power of the Spirit entities when they see an actual surgery and witness how it happens: no anesthesia, no pain, almost no bleeding, essentially no scars remaining from the incision, and formidable-looking tools that do not harm the patient.

The hypothesis may very well explain this if one looks at it as a two-stage process: *first* the actual visible procedure (i.e., incision, the scraping of the eye with a simple knife, or the insertion of a long metal tool up though the nostrils), and *then* to the actual "work" on the pathological tissue.

The first stage would be an enormous effort—again via directed contraction and expansion sequences of the energy field of Spirit emanations—for no other reason but to *demonstrate* that it is possible for Spirit entities to do all this. Taking care of the incision, no bleeding, no pain, no need for anesthesia, the strange phenomenon regarding the transformation of the metal tools into some other pliable substance—all this would happen in accordance with the hypothesis of an almost endless string of molecular-level events due to a super-fast chain of Spirit-guided contractions and expansions of energetic Spirit-emanated spheres. All this would be done to "disguise" and/or "deactivate" the physical impact on the patient of the crude incisions done by the healer in this "visible" part of the surgery.

The second stage would be the actual act of healing, as described earlier for "regular" invisible surgeries. This second stage would really not be in any reasonable way connected with the first stage. The first stage would be only to satisfy human curiosity; the second would be the true act of healing from whatever ailment the patient is afflicted.

This would also explain why the few types of visible surgeries practiced at the Casa are administered for *any* kind of ailment. Be it an incision in the abdomen, the scraping of an eye, or the insertion of the metal instrument up into the nose and turning it around several times, the method John of God selects appears to be entirely random with regard to the specific ailment the patient may be suffering from.

• • •

Many of us have witnessed incredible events of spiritual healing occurring around persons like Ron Roth, John of God, Sri Bhagavan, and numerous others. While the evidence is hard to deny in and of itself, our inability to fathom a mechanism for such healings to occur often tends to lead us into disbelief even in the face of the best evidence. The study of the orbs gives rise to a "mechanism" for spiritual healing, still simplistic, yet quite feasible.

It is certainly presumptuous to infer that we now have an explanation for spiritual healing. But the orbs do indicate that there is a connection between the Spiritual reality and our health. In fact, it may well be even more presumptuous to think that conventional medications or even physical surgery in and by themselves provide healing from ailments. We do not live in a reality that ends where our ability to see, hear, sense, calculate, think, and communicate ends; we are participants in a system that extends infinitely beyond those limitations. Its energy is boundless, and its healing capacity is unlimited. The question is only whether or not we make use of it. The solution cannot be found in one *or* the other, but in one *and* the other.

Bibliography

Azevedo, José Lacerda de. *Spirit and Matter: New Horizons for Medicine.* Tempe, Ariz.: New Falcon Publications, 1997.

Browne, Sylvia. *Prophecy: What the Future Holds for You.* New York: New American Library, 2005.

Heinemann, Klaus. *Consciousness or Entrophy?: A Guide Toward a Fresh Understanding of Man's Purpose and Required Response.* Sunnyvale, Calif.: Eloret Press, 1991. (Out of print; copies still available from the author.)

————. *Expanding Perception.* Tarentum, Pa.: Word Association Publishers, 2004.

Kuhlman, Kathryn. See http://www.godswordtowomen.org/studies/articles/kuhlman.htm.

Laurentin, René, and Henri Joyeux. *Scientific and Medical Studies on the Apparitions at Medjugorje.* Dublin: Veritas Publishing, 1987. (Original in French by Editions OEIL, Paris, 1985.)

Martin III, Harvey J. *The Secret Teachings of the Espiritistas: A Hidden History of Spiritual Healing.* Savannah, Ga.: Metamind Publications, 1999.

McPherson, Aimee Semple. See http://en.wikipedia.org/wiki/Aimee_Semple_McPherson.

Rathbun, Harry. *Creative Initiative: Guide to Fulfillment.* Palo Alto, Calif.: Creative Initiative Foundation, 1976.

Roth, Ron, with Peter Occhiogrosso. *The Healing Path of Prayer: A Modern Mystic's Guide to Spiritual Power.* New York: Harmony Books, 1997.

Roth, Ron. *Holy Spirit for Healing: Merging Ancient Wisdom with Modern Medicine.* Carlsbad, Calif.: Hay House, 2001.

————. *Holy Spirit: The Boundless Energy of God.* Carlsbad, Calif.: Hay House, 2000.

————. *Prayer and the Five Stages of Healing.* Carlsbad, Calif.: Hay House, 1999.

Sweet, Leonore. *How to Photograph the Paranormal.* Charlottesville, Va.: Hampton Roads Publishing, 2005.

Tiller, William A. "A Gas Discharge Device for Investigating Focused Human Attention." *Journal of Scientific Exploration* 4, no. 2 (1990), 255.

Tiller, William A., Walter E. Dibble, and J. Gregory Fandel. *Some Science Adventures with Real Magic.* Walnut Creek, Calif.: Pavior Publishing, 2005.

Xavier, André Luiz Francisco Candido. *The Astral City.* Electronic edition at http://www.sgny.org/main/Books/AstralCity.pdf.

Authors' Conclusion

At the onset of the venture of publicizing the results of our individual research on orbs jointly in this book, we had posed two key questions: (1) whether these features that ended up caught in our cameras by the tens of thousands are for real, and (2) whether they might be connected with realities that are outside of normal human perception. The rapidly growing multitude of orb sightings worldwide made it exceedingly important for these questions to be investigated.

We strongly felt that the answers would likely be affirmative, even though there was surprisingly little overlap in our research approach. We were also like-minded in our expectation that, if the orb phenomenon were indeed connected with a supernatural realm, there would be important follow-up questions to be addressed. Are we dealing with entities from what is commonly perceived as the divine realm? Are these orbs related to life elsewhere in our universe? Is there a teaching or a message? What is there to be learned from our findings?

Our results show many commonalities and interesting differences. Probably the most significant differences between our observations stem from, and are related to, our experimental approaches. Míceál predominantly used out-of-doors situations, mostly involving very few people, while Klaus concentrated on indoor occasions, predominantly during the presence of large groupings of people in spiritual retreat settings.

Irrespective of these almost diametrically opposed experimental conditions, our findings agree in many aspects, including

- Use of a flash is all but essential in photographing orbs.
- This may be because the means by which they are recorded on the CCD of the camera is not through reflection or scattering but through fluorescence.
- Orbs are abundantly present, and the frequency of their showings has significantly increased since our research started.
- The argument of skeptics that orb photographs must all be due to some kind of experimental deficiency cannot be upheld.
- There is no indication that orbs are diffraction effects at physical objects.
- There is no evidence that orbs are images of physical objects.
- There is no compelling theory/argument at this time that would explain the energy of orbs to be of the type of "conventional" physical electromagnetic waves or plasmas.
- Yet orbs are energetic phenomena.
- Orbs appear to be showing up at randomly different locations in series of pictures.
- There are multitudes of varieties of orbs.
- Often, orbs of predominantly one variety show in any one setting.
- Orbs show signs of intelligence.
- Orbs appear to want to communicate with us.
- We could not find any adverse intent from orbs toward us; in fact, their way of exhibiting their presence hinted toward unconditional benevolence.

- The evidence from orb fluorescence poses the question as to whether these frequency realms detected through that process may actually be realms just as solid within themselves as our reality is "solid" to us.
- If these hypotheses are true, many of the conventional understandings of matters such as "spirit" and "the beyond" will need redefinition.

From these observations we conclude that our two principal questions are to be answered in the affirmative: Orbs are for real, and they are connected with realms that are outside of normal human perception. They appear to function outside the conventional laws of physics, yet they can communicate with us through digital cameras that are now readily available to everybody.

This communication appears to be initiated by them, and we thus are safe to conclude that it is driven by a specific purpose and intent. We have each advanced certain hypotheses that address what there might be to learn from the orb phenomenon at this time, but we concur that the real answers to this important question are likely still outstanding.

Whereas the research presented in this book is likely based on the largest body of evidence ever to date assembled on the orb phenomenon, we feel that we have just scratched the surface of what this all means. More research will have to follow and will yield more insight. The question of the meaning behind the phenomenon is still almost entirely unanswered, and some of the hypotheses we have "bravely" formulated in order to get the discussion going are still just that—hypotheses.

We look forward to an exciting continuation of the quest into the orb phenomenon and invite your participation!

Míceál Ledwith, D.D., LL.D.
Klaus Heinemann, Ph.D.

To learn more about this amazing phenomenon, order *Orbs: The Veil is Lifting*, the DVD featuring commentary from authors Klaus Heinemann and Míceál Ledwith, along with other experts on the subject of orbs.

$29.95 US / $34.00 Can, 63 minutes

Purchase directly from Beyond Words Publishing Inc. or from your local bookstore.

20827 N.W. Cornell Road, Suite 500
Hillsboro, OR 97124-98908
503-531-8700
www.beyondword.com
or email us at info@beyondword.com